CSSLP
Complete Self-Assessment G

The guidance in this Self-Assessment is based on CSSLP best practices and standards in business process architecture, design and quality management. The guidance is also based on the professional judgment of the individual collaborators listed in the Acknowledgments.

Notice of rights

Trademarks

Table of Contents

About The Art of Service

The Art of Service, Business Process Architects since 2000, is dedicated to helping stakeholders achieve excellence.

Defining, designing, creating, and implementing a process to solve a stakeholders challenge or meet an objective is the most valuable role... In EVERY group, company, organization and department.

Unless you're talking a one-time, single-use project, there should be a process. Whether that process is managed and implemented by humans, AI, or a combination of the two, it needs to be designed by someone with a complex enough perspective to ask the right questions.

Someone capable of asking the right questions and step back and say, 'What are we really trying to accomplish here? And is there a different way to look at it?'

With The Art of Service's Standard Requirements Self-Assessments, we empower people who can do just that — whether their title is marketer, entrepreneur, manager, salesperson, consultant, Business Process Manager, executive assistant, IT Manager, CIO etc... —they are the people who rule the future. They are people who watch the process as it happens, and ask the right questions to make the process work better.

Contact us when you need any support with this Self-Assessment and any help with templates, blue-prints and examples of standard documents you might need:

http://theartofservice.com
service@theartofservice.com

Acknowledgments

This checklist was developed under the auspices of The Art of Service, chaired by Gerardus Blokdyk.

Representatives from several client companies participated in the preparation of this Self-Assessment.

In addition, we are thankful for the design and printing services provided.

Included Resources - how to access

Included with your purchase of the book is the CSSLP Self-Assessment Spreadsheet Dashboard which contains all questions and Self-Assessment areas and auto-generates insights, graphs, and project RACI planning - all with examples to get you started right away.

How? Simply send an email to
access@theartofservice.com
with this books' title in the subject to get the CSSLP Self Assessment Tool right away.

You will receive the following contents with New and Updated specific criteria:

• The latest quick edition of the book in PDF

• The latest complete edition of the book in PDF, which criteria correspond to the criteria in...

• The Self-Assessment Excel Dashboard, and...

• Example pre-filled Self-Assessment Excel Dashboard to get familiar with results generation

• In-depth specific Checklists covering the topic

• Project management checklists and templates to assist with implementation

INCLUDES LIFETIME SELF ASSESSMENT UPDATES

Every self assessment comes with Lifetime Updates and Lifetime Free Updated Books. Lifetime Updates is an industry-first feature which allows you to receive verified self assessment updates, ensuring you always have the most accurate information at your fingertips.

Get it now- you will be glad you did - do it now, before you forget.

Send an email to **access@theartofservice.com** with this books' title in the subject to get the CSSLP Self Assessment Tool right away.

Your feedback is invaluable to us

If you recently bought this book, we would love to hear from you! You can do this by writing a review on amazon (or the online store where you purchased this book) about your last purchase! As part of our continual service improvement process, we love to hear real client experiences and feedback.

How does it work?
To post a review on Amazon, just log in to your account and click on the Create Your Own Review button (under Customer Reviews) of the relevant product page. You can find examples of product reviews in Amazon. If you purchased from another online store, simply follow their procedures.

What happens when I submit my review?
Once you have submitted your review, send us an email at review@theartofservice.com with the link to your review so we can properly thank you for your feedback.

Purpose of this Self-Assessment

This Self-Assessment has been developed to improve understanding of the requirements and elements of CSSLP, based on best practices and standards in business process architecture, design and quality management.

It is designed to allow for a rapid Self-Assessment to determine how closely existing management practices and procedures correspond to the elements of the Self-Assessment.

The criteria of requirements and elements of CSSLP have been rephrased in the format of a Self-Assessment questionnaire, with a seven-criterion scoring system, as explained in this document.

In this format, even with limited background knowledge of CSSLP, a manager can quickly review existing operations to determine how they measure up to the standards. This in turn can serve as the starting point of a 'gap analysis' to identify management tools or system elements that might usefully be implemented in the organization to help improve overall performance.

How to use the Self-Assessment

On the following pages are a series of questions to identify to what extent your CSSLP initiative is complete in comparison to the requirements set in standards.

To facilitate answering the questions, there is a space in front of each question to enter a score on a scale of '1' to '5'.

1 Strongly Disagree

2 Disagree

3 Neutral

4 Agree

5 Strongly Agree

Read the question and rate it with the following in front of mind:

'In my belief,
the answer to this question is clearly defined'.

There are two ways in which you can choose to interpret this statement;
1. how aware are you that the answer to the question is clearly defined
2. for more in-depth analysis you can choose to gather evidence and confirm the answer to the question. This obviously will take more time, most Self-Assessment

users opt for the first way to interpret the question and dig deeper later on based on the outcome of the overall Self-Assessment.

A score of '1' would mean that the answer is not clear at all, where a '5' would mean the answer is crystal clear and defined. Leave emtpy when the question is not applicable or you don't want to answer it, you can skip it without affecting your score. Write your score in the space provided.

After you have responded to all the appropriate statements in each section, compute your average score for that section, using the formula provided, and round to the nearest tenth. Then transfer to the corresponding spoke in the CSSLP Scorecard on the second next page of the Self-Assessment.

Your completed CSSLP Scorecard will give you a clear presentation of which CSSLP areas need attention.

CSSLP
Scorecard Example

Example of how the finalized Scorecard can look like:

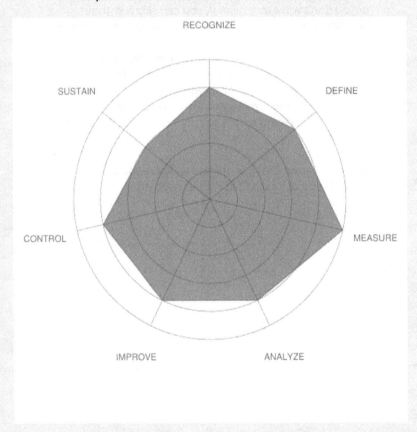

CSSLP
Scorecard

Your Scores:

RECOGNIZE

SUSTAIN

DEFINE

CONTROL

MEASURE

IMPROVE

ANALYZE

BEGINNING OF THE SELF-ASSESSMENT:

CRITERION #1: RECOGNIZE

INTENT: Be aware of the need for change. Recognize that there is an unfavorable variation, problem or symptom.

In my belief, the answer to this question is clearly defined:

5 Strongly Agree

4 Agree

3 Neutral

2 Disagree

1 Strongly Disagree

1. Who is the person or role that will review users rights and how often they will needed to do that?
<--- Score

2. What does CSSLP success mean to the stakeholders?
<--- Score

3. What tools and technologies are needed for a

custom CSSLP project?

<--- Score

4. How can auditing be a preventative security measure?

<--- Score

5. What is the smallest subset of the problem you can usefully solve?

<--- Score

6. How can you recognize malware & share that info?

<--- Score

7. Who else hopes to benefit from it?

<--- Score

8. What effect could a event have on maintenance performance, and what is its expected influence on software quality from the perspective of the customer?

<--- Score

9. What is reported as causing any kind of software problem?

<--- Score

10. When a CSSLP manager recognizes a problem, what options are available?

<--- Score

11. Will new equipment/products be required to facilitate CSSLP delivery, for example is new software needed?

<--- Score

12. What is the typical vehicle downtime for regular preventative maintenance checks?

<--- Score

13. What type of person is needed for software maintenance?

<--- Score

14. Determine the storage requirements (how long do you need to be able to store logs for)?

<--- Score

15. How are manufacturer warranties and complimentary services incorporated into preventative maintenance services?

<--- Score

16. What exactly do you need to accomplish?

<--- Score

17. Will a response program recognize when a crisis occurs and provide some level of response?

<--- Score

18. How will issues be reported and handled?

<--- Score

19. What is the product and why do you need it?

<--- Score

20. How much are sponsors, customers, partners, stakeholders involved in CSSLP? In other words, what are the risks, if CSSLP does not deliver successfully?

<--- Score

21. How are the CSSLP's objectives aligned to the group's overall stakeholder strategy?
<--- Score

22. Are there CSSLP problems defined?
<--- Score

23. Are there recognized CSSLP problems?
<--- Score

24. What should be considered when identifying available resources, constraints, and deadlines?
<--- Score

25. How do you assess your CSSLP workforce capability and capacity needs, including skills, competencies, and staffing levels?
<--- Score

26. What would happen if CSSLP weren't done?
<--- Score

27. Who defines the rules in relation to any given issue?
<--- Score

28. What has been done before to solve a problem similar to this one?
<--- Score

29. What do you need to start doing?
<--- Score

30. What problems are you facing and how do you consider CSSLP will circumvent those obstacles?
<--- Score

31. As a sponsor, customer or management, how important is it to meet goals, objectives?
<--- Score

32. Sdn security issues: how secure is the sdn stack?
<--- Score

33. Can you prevent and/or detect manual override of this feature by the user?
<--- Score

34. Hardware and software; is the recovery site equipped with the precise computer hardware and software that the institution needs to continue operations?
<--- Score

35. Configuration management and auditing; can you identify just what changed from version 3.2 to version 3.3 of a module?
<--- Score

36. How does it fit into your organizational needs and tasks?
<--- Score

37. Can management personnel recognize the monetary benefit of CSSLP?
<--- Score

38. How do you take a forward-looking perspective in identifying CSSLP research related to market response and models?
<--- Score

39. Does the design meet the problem requirements?

<--- Score

40. How are you going to measure success?

<--- Score

41. Key staff identified; what happens if others leave?

<--- Score

42. Is it now an operational system that satisfies users needs?

<--- Score

43. Are there any specific expectations or concerns about the CSSLP team, CSSLP itself?

<--- Score

44. What information do users need?

<--- Score

45. What situation(s) led to this CSSLP Self Assessment?

<--- Score

46. Hardware and Software-Is the recovery site equipped with the precise computer hardware and software that your organization needs to continue operations?

<--- Score

47. Is it clear when you think of the day ahead of you what activities and tasks you need to complete?

<--- Score

48. What objects does the application need?
<--- Score

49. What – Scope. What exactly do you need to accomplish?
<--- Score

50. Key staff identified what happens if they leave?
<--- Score

51. Does CSSLP create potential expectations in other areas that need to be recognized and considered?
<--- Score

52. What are the expected benefits of CSSLP to the stakeholder?
<--- Score

53. What vendors make products that address the CSSLP needs?
<--- Score

54. What are the stakeholder objectives to be achieved with CSSLP?
<--- Score

Add up total points for this section:
_ _ _ _ _ = Total points for this section

Divided by: _ _ _ _ _ _ (number of statements answered) = _ _ _ _ _ _
Average score for this section

Transfer your score to the CSSLP Index at the beginning of the Self-

Assessment.

CRITERION #2: DEFINE:

INTENT: Formulate the stakeholder problem. Define the problem, needs and objectives.

In my belief, the answer to this question is clearly defined:

5 Strongly Agree

4 Agree

3 Neutral

2 Disagree

1 Strongly Disagree

1. Has anyone else (internal or external to the group) attempted to solve this problem or a similar one before? If so, what knowledge can be leveraged from these previous efforts?
<--- Score

2. How is the team tracking and documenting its work?
<--- Score

3. Is full participation by members in regularly held team meetings guaranteed?
<--- Score

4. Is the team equipped with available and reliable resources?
<--- Score

5. Is CSSLP linked to key stakeholder goals and objectives?
<--- Score

6. How was the 'as is' process map developed, reviewed, verified and validated?
<--- Score

7. Has everyone on the team, including the team leaders, been properly trained?
<--- Score

8. Is there a completed, verified, and validated high-level 'as is' (not 'should be' or 'could be') stakeholder process map?
<--- Score

9. What training does your company offer related to defining security requirements, secure architecture and design, secure coding practices, and security testing?
<--- Score

10. When do you have to pay attention to the security requirements of your information system?
<--- Score

11. Will team members regularly document their CSSLP work?
<--- Score

12. What are the record-keeping requirements of CSSLP activities?
<--- Score

13. Is the team sponsored by a champion or stakeholder leader?
<--- Score

14. What security requirements are incorporated into SDLC?
<--- Score

15. Are team charters developed?
<--- Score

16. Is there a completed SIPOC representation, describing the Suppliers, Inputs, Process, Outputs, and Customers?
<--- Score

17. In what step in the SDLC do you define business requirements?
<--- Score

18. Have the customer needs been translated into specific, measurable requirements? How?
<--- Score

19. Will team members perform CSSLP work when assigned and in a timely fashion?
<--- Score

20. What are the Roles and Responsibilities for each team member and its leadership? Where is this documented?
<--- Score

21. How will variation in the actual durations of each activity be dealt with to ensure that the expected CSSLP results are met?
<--- Score

22. Is there a CSSLP management charter, including stakeholder case, problem and goal statements, scope, milestones, roles and responsibilities, communication plan?
<--- Score

23. Are stakeholder processes mapped?
<--- Score

24. Does the maintenance requirement for the client software for your CM tool provide the capability to be remotely installed and updated over a Local Area Network (LAN) or Wide Area Network (WAN)?
<--- Score

25. Is there a critical path to deliver CSSLP results?
<--- Score

26. What are the dynamics of the communication plan?
<--- Score

27. Are customer(s) identified and segmented according to their different needs and requirements?
<--- Score

28. How do you define a policy of secure configurations?
<--- Score

29. How and when will the baselines be defined?
<--- Score

30. Is the current 'as is' process being followed? If not, what are the discrepancies?
<--- Score

31. What baselines are required to be defined and managed?
<--- Score

32. Have you completed all the required checklists?
<--- Score

33. Have specific policy objectives been defined?
<--- Score

34. Is a fully trained team formed, supported, and committed to work on the CSSLP improvements?
<--- Score

35. What sources do you use to gather information for a CSSLP study?
<--- Score

36. Are customers identified and high impact areas defined?
<--- Score

37. Are there different segments of customers?

<--- Score

38. Are different versions of process maps needed to account for the different types of inputs?
<--- Score

39. What critical content must be communicated – who, what, when, where, and how?
<--- Score

40. Has a project plan, Gantt chart, or similar been developed/completed?
<--- Score

41. Is requirements (or design, or coding, or etc.) a phase or an activity?
<--- Score

42. How do you write test cases?
<--- Score

43. Has a team charter been developed and communicated?
<--- Score

44. Is data collected and displayed to better understand customer(s) critical needs and requirements.
<--- Score

45. How did the CSSLP manager receive input to the development of a CSSLP improvement plan and the estimated completion dates/times of each activity?
<--- Score

46. Are there any constraints known that bear on

the ability to perform CSSLP work? How is the team
addressing them?
<--- Score

47. What are CMM levels and their definitions?
<--- Score

**48. Which parts of the requirements and design
are unclear or poorly thought out?**
<--- Score

**49. Which participants are required in a security
assessment?**
<--- Score

**50. What validation criteria are required to define
a success system?**
<--- Score

51. What are the boundaries of the scope? What is in
bounds and what is not? What is the start point? What
is the stop point?
<--- Score

52. Is the team adequately staffed with the desired
cross-functionality? If not, what additional resources
are available to the team?
<--- Score

53. What constraints exist that might impact the
team?
<--- Score

54. How can the value of CSSLP be defined?
<--- Score

55. Is CSSLP required?
<--- Score

56. How will the CSSLP team and the group measure complete success of CSSLP?
<--- Score

57. What customer feedback methods were used to solicit their input?
<--- Score

58. Are improvement team members fully trained on CSSLP?
<--- Score

59. Monolithic configurations no longer required -- how do you manage site specific configurations?
<--- Score

60. What specifically is the problem? Where does it occur? When does it occur? What is its extent?
<--- Score

61. Do you require external user authentication (via Active Directory, SSO, or Token) ?
<--- Score

62. How do you define a service?
<--- Score

63. What is the definition of top down design?
<--- Score

64. Are the requirements clear and unambiguous?
<--- Score

65. What systems are required to support the strategic goals of your organization?
<--- Score

66. What are the rough order estimates on cost savings/opportunities that CSSLP brings?
<--- Score

67. Is there regularly 100% attendance at the team meetings? If not, have appointed substitutes attended to preserve cross-functionality and full representation?
<--- Score

68. Is there a requirement that system and application logs be stored on a separate server?
<--- Score

69. What is the definition of top down design in your organization?
<--- Score

70. If substitutes have been appointed, have they been briefed on the CSSLP goals and received regular communications as to the progress to date?
<--- Score

71. Are roles and responsibilities formally defined?
<--- Score

72. Has the CSSLP work been fairly and/or equitably divided and delegated among team members who are qualified and capable to perform the work? Has everyone contributed?
<--- Score

73. When is the estimated completion date?
<--- Score

74. Do you require a DBA (on a full or part time basis)?
<--- Score

75. Is the team formed and are team leaders (Coaches and Management Leads) assigned?
<--- Score

76. Does the team have regular meetings?
<--- Score

77. What is the definition of bottom up design?
<--- Score

78. How do you keep key subject matter experts in the loop?
<--- Score

79. How will it be verified that the product performs as required?
<--- Score

80. Is the CSSLP scope manageable?
<--- Score

81. Will application level logs be required and what is the required retention period?
<--- Score

82. How does the CSSLP manager ensure against scope creep?
<--- Score

83. Are accountability and ownership for CSSLP clearly defined?
<--- Score

84. Has the direction changed at all during the course of CSSLP? If so, when did it change and why?
<--- Score

85. Do the problem and goal statements meet the SMART criteria (specific, measurable, attainable, relevant, and time-bound)?
<--- Score

86. What level of detail is required in the logs?
<--- Score

87. What would be the goal or target for a CSSLP's improvement team?
<--- Score

88. Has the improvement team collected the 'voice of the customer' (obtained feedback – qualitative and quantitative)?
<--- Score

89. When are meeting minutes sent out? Who is on the distribution list?
<--- Score

90. Who are the CSSLP improvement team members, including Management Leads and Coaches?
<--- Score

91. Has/have the customer(s) been identified?
<--- Score

92. How would you define CSSLP leadership?
<--- Score

93. What are the compelling stakeholder reasons for embarking on CSSLP?
<--- Score

94. Will the software/work require maintenance?
<--- Score

95. Is CSSLP currently on schedule according to the plan?
<--- Score

96. Has a high-level 'as is' process map been completed, verified and validated?
<--- Score

97. What work products should be examined for defects?
<--- Score

98. Are approval levels defined for contracts and supplements to contracts?
<--- Score

99. Is it clearly defined in and to your organization what you do?
<--- Score

100. Are records management requirements incorporated into the system?
<--- Score

101. How do you gather requirements and how accurate are they?

<--- Score

102. Is the improvement team aware of the different versions of a process: what they think it is vs. what it actually is vs. what it should be vs. what it could be?
<--- Score

103. What key stakeholder process output measure(s) does CSSLP leverage and how?
<--- Score

104. When is/was the CSSLP start date?
<--- Score

105. What defines best in class?
<--- Score

106. How often are the team meetings?
<--- Score

107. Whats a test case?
<--- Score

Add up total points for this section:
_____ = Total points for this section

Divided by: _____ (number of statements answered) = _____
Average score for this section

Transfer your score to the CSSLP Index at the beginning of the Self-Assessment.

CRITERION #3: MEASURE:

In my belief, the answer to this question is clearly defined:

5 Strongly Agree

4 Agree

3 Neutral

2 Disagree

1 Strongly Disagree

1. What are the key input variables? What are the key process variables? What are the key output variables? <--- Score

2. Are missed CSSLP opportunities costing your organization money? <--- Score

3. How do you estimate software maintenance

cost?
<--- Score

4. What are the costs associated with updating existing hardware, firmware, software, and applications versus the costs of adding entirely new elements for a totally new security posture?
<--- Score

5. How are measurements made?
<--- Score

6. Which functionality has the largest financial impact on users?
<--- Score

7. Who should receive measurement reports?
<--- Score

8. What stage of bug fixing is the most cost effective?
<--- Score

9. Is long term and short term variability accounted for?
<--- Score

10. What methods are feasible and acceptable to estimate the impact of reforms?
<--- Score

11. How do you identify and analyze stakeholders and their interests?
<--- Score

12. What are the agreed upon definitions of the high

impact areas, defect(s), unit(s), and opportunities that will figure into the process capability metrics?
<--- Score

13. Which functionality has the largest safety impact?
<--- Score

14. Among the CSSLP product and service cost to be estimated, which is considered hardest to estimate?
<--- Score

15. Penetration tests are sometimes called white hat attacks because in a pen test, the good guys are attempting to break in. What are the different categories of penetration testing your organization performs?
<--- Score

16. How do you control the overall costs of your work processes?
<--- Score

17. Is the solution cost-effective?
<--- Score

18. What measurements are being captured?
<--- Score

19. What are your customers expectations and measures?
<--- Score

20. Can you measure the return on analysis?
<--- Score

21. Is data collection planned and executed?
<--- Score

22. What impact would there be on your operations is the system was unavailable?
<--- Score

23. What data was collected (past, present, future/ ongoing)?
<--- Score

24. Where is it measured?
<--- Score

25. What tools and methods are used to measure the defects?
<--- Score

26. Are contingencies identified if this activity can't be completed on time, what is the impact on other activities?
<--- Score

27. Is there a Performance Baseline?
<--- Score

28. How can your organization remove a piece of software from a production setting, without impacting the overall functionality of an application, software suite, or system?
<--- Score

29. Is Process Variation Displayed/Communicated?
<--- Score

30. What particular quality tools did the team find

helpful in establishing measurements?
<--- Score

31. Was a data collection plan established?
<--- Score

32. What are the costs of reform?
<--- Score

33. What is an unallowable cost?
<--- Score

34. How do you measure the success of your implementations?
<--- Score

35. What has the team done to assure the stability and accuracy of the measurement process?
<--- Score

36. Have all non-recommended alternatives been analyzed in sufficient detail?
<--- Score

37. What is the difference between priority and severity?
<--- Score

38. How can you measure the performance?
<--- Score

39. Does CSSLP analysis isolate the fundamental causes of problems?
<--- Score

40. What measurements are possible, practicable and

meaningful?

<--- Score

41. Are the units of measure consistent?

<--- Score

42. Are process variation components displayed/
communicated using suitable charts, graphs, plots?

<--- Score

**43. What are the potential areas of conflict that
can arise between organisations IT and marketing
functions around the deployment and use of
business intelligence and data analytics software
services and whats the best way to resolve them?**

<--- Score

44. Who should measure software productivity?

<--- Score

45. Who participated in the data collection for
measurements?

<--- Score

46. Does your organization systematically track and
analyze outcomes related for accountability and
quality improvement?

<--- Score

47. How will success or failure be measured?

<--- Score

48. Is key measure data collection planned
and executed, process variation displayed and
communicated and performance baselined?

<--- Score

49. What to measure?
<--- Score

50. How do you measure lifecycle phases?
<--- Score

51. Whats the difference between priority and severity?
<--- Score

52. How can the documentation and analysis of the ALM solution be facilitated in an organisation operating in a global software development environment?
<--- Score

53. Does the SDLC process incorporate the cost of security at every step as required?
<--- Score

54. What kinds of problems would cause the most Customer Service complaints?
<--- Score

55. What is the right balance of time and resources between investigation, analysis, and discussion and dissemination?
<--- Score

56. What charts has the team used to display the components of variation in the process?
<--- Score

57. Are high impact defects defined and identified in the stakeholder process?

<--- Score

58. What do you measure and why?
<--- Score

59. What are the types and number of measures to use?
<--- Score

60. What kinds of problems would cause the worst publicity?
<--- Score

61. What exactly is expected in regression analysis?
<--- Score

62. How do you know that any CSSLP analysis is complete and comprehensive?
<--- Score

63. How can you measure CSSLP in a systematic way?
<--- Score

64. How do you focus on what is right -not who is right?
<--- Score

65. Do staff have the necessary skills to collect, analyze, and report data?
<--- Score

66. Are there checkpoints throughout the software development life cycle (SDLC) verifying and certifying that the security requirements are being met?

<--- Score

67. Do you effectively measure and reward individual and team performance?
<--- Score

68. In which SDLC phase will the analyst study your organizations current procedures and the information systems used to perform tasks?
<--- Score

69. What potential environmental factors impact the CSSLP effort?
<--- Score

70. How is performance measured?
<--- Score

71. Do you purchase software licenses or maintenance at high costs?
<--- Score

72. Can you think of any other benefits of bringing the security focus from the end of the software development lifecycle to the beginning?
<--- Score

73. What are the uncertainties surrounding estimates of impact?
<--- Score

74. How will your organization measure success?
<--- Score

75. What causes data validity errors?
<--- Score

76. Are key measures identified and agreed upon?
<--- Score

77. How frequently do you track CSSLP measures?
<--- Score

78. What are the benefits and costs of early user involvement compared to usability testing?
<--- Score

79. If contingencies identified if this activity can't be completed on time, what is the impact on other activities?
<--- Score

80. What Measures Do Vendors Use for Software Assurance?
<--- Score

81. How large is the gap between current performance and the customer-specified (goal) performance?
<--- Score

82. Have you found any 'ground fruit' or 'low-hanging fruit' for immediate remedies to the gap in performance?
<--- Score

83. When will the Program Offices know what the priorities are for a Fiscal Year (FY)?
<--- Score

84. What is your measure for determining if the quality of the software is degrading?

<--- Score

85. How do you aggregate measures across priorities?
<--- Score

86. How does your company ensure competitive costs for labor, maintenance and repair parts, and equipment?
<--- Score

87. Does CSSLP analysis show the relationships among important CSSLP factors?
<--- Score

88. What are your key CSSLP indicators that you will measure, analyze and track?
<--- Score

89. What key measures identified indicate the performance of the stakeholder process?
<--- Score

90. Does CSSLP systematically track and analyze outcomes for accountability and quality improvement?
<--- Score

91. Is data collected on key measures that were identified?
<--- Score

92. Is a solid data collection plan established that includes measurement systems analysis?
<--- Score

93. Which aspects of similar/related previous

projects caused problems?

<--- Score

94. The approach of traditional CSSLP works for detail complexity but is focused on a systematic approach rather than an understanding of the nature of systems themselves, what approach will permit your organization to deal with the kind of unpredictable emergent behaviors that dynamic complexity can introduce?

<--- Score

Add up total points for this section:

_____ = Total points for this section

Divided by: _____ (number of statements answered) = _____ Average score for this section

Transfer your score to the CSSLP Index at the beginning of the Self-Assessment.

CRITERION #4: ANALYZE:

INTENT: Analyze causes, assumptions
and hypotheses.

In my belief, the answer to this
question is clearly defined:

5 Strongly Agree

4 Agree

3 Neutral

2 Disagree

1 Strongly Disagree

1. Is the CSSLP process severely broken such that a re-design is necessary?
<--- Score

2. List the process for removing a user from the system?
<--- Score

3. What process should you select for improvement?
<--- Score

4. What are your current levels and trends in key CSSLP measures or indicators of product and process performance that are important to and directly serve your customers?
<--- Score

5. Was a cause-and-effect diagram used to explore the different types of causes (or sources of variation)?
<--- Score

6. What other jobs or tasks affect the performance of the steps in the CSSLP process?
<--- Score

7. Identify an operational issue in your organization. for example, could a particular task be done more quickly or more efficiently by CSSLP?
<--- Score

8. Does management use a formal methodology or process to guide the acquisition, development, or maintenance of new or modified software?
<--- Score

9. How will the computer, software, databases and other technology utilized to perform work be secured and protected from use by other individuals?
<--- Score

10. What areas of the business are you going to take data from?
<--- Score

11. Have manual calculations, manual data entry,

or human adjustments to software settings been checked?

<--- Score

12. Software-defined networking: radical simplification of the data center, or just smoke and mirrors?

<--- Score

13. What are the roles of the Contractors in the maintenance process?

<--- Score

14. All software releases referenced in the What Products and Services Are Required to Adopt the Security Development Lifecycle Process?

<--- Score

15. Do your leaders quickly bounce back from setbacks?

<--- Score

16. What controls do you have in place to protect data?

<--- Score

17. Is data and process analysis, root cause analysis and quantifying the gap/opportunity in place?

<--- Score

18. How is the way you as the leader think and process information affecting your organizational culture?

<--- Score

19. Are you ready for the software-defined datacentre?

<--- Score

20. Is your organization Records Officer included from the beginning in the system design process?
<--- Score

21. What are the data backup policies and procedures?
<--- Score

22. Who authorizes access to the system and data?
<--- Score

23. How is test data handled?
<--- Score

24. What were the crucial 'moments of truth' on the process map?
<--- Score

25. Were any designed experiments used to generate additional insight into the data analysis?
<--- Score

26. When conducting a business process reengineering study, what do you look for when trying to identify business processes to change?
<--- Score

27. Will the Big Data cloud environment support scale-out, shared-nothing massively parallel processing, storage optimization, dynamic query optimization, and mixed workload management better than alternative deployment models (e.g., on-premises appliances, software on commodity hardware)?

<--- Score

28. What is the difference between data validity and data integrity?
<--- Score

29. How will test data be provided?
<--- Score

30. Does your organization currently use a formal decision-making process to make equipment maintenance, repair, and/or replacement decisions on individual pieces of equipment?
<--- Score

31. How was the detailed process map generated, verified, and validated?
<--- Score

32. Did any additional data need to be collected?
<--- Score

33. Why should users be involved in the change process?
<--- Score

34. What are the drivers of software maintenance?
<--- Score

35. What does the data say about the performance of the stakeholder process?
<--- Score

36. Have any additional benefits been identified that will result from closing all or most of the gaps?
<--- Score

37. What security design and security architecture documents are prepared as part of the SDLC process?

<--- Score

38. Were Pareto charts (or similar) used to portray the 'heavy hitters' (or key sources of variation)?

<--- Score

39. Does quantified terms mean including the data demonstrating the pass or fail for a test?

<--- Score

40. What is the process for defining a defect as Warranty?

<--- Score

41. What tools were used to narrow the list of possible causes?

<--- Score

42. What products are you going to be taking log data from?

<--- Score

43. Is the software and application development process based on an industry best practice and is information security included throughout the software development life cycle (SDLC) process?

<--- Score

44. Is the suppliers process defined and controlled?

<--- Score

45. Do you count or measure concurrent use;

installations per device or processor; user; Web use; VM?
<--- Score

46. Were there any improvement opportunities identified from the process analysis?
<--- Score

47. Are gaps between current performance and the goal performance identified?
<--- Score

48. What information is to be processed?
<--- Score

49. Which processes does risk assessment include?
<--- Score

50. What is the process for creating Business Requirements Documents (BRDs)?
<--- Score

51. Since encryption actually transforms the data, how is this expected to be validated?
<--- Score

52. Have the problem and goal statements been updated to reflect the additional knowledge gained from the analyze phase?
<--- Score

53. How do you measure the operational performance of your key work systems and processes, including productivity, cycle time, and other appropriate measures of process effectiveness, efficiency, and innovation?

<--- Score

54. Do you take responsibility to set up a QA infrastructure/process, testing and quality of the entire product?
<--- Score

55. Was a detailed process map created to amplify critical steps of the 'as is' stakeholder process?
<--- Score

56. Are you using an external virtualization technology to achieve database consolidation, and if yes, are the performance and complexity of operations acceptable?
<--- Score

57. How does the organization define, manage, and improve its CSSLP processes?
<--- Score

58. How are determinations made as to which data from the survey is relevant to the organizations operations?
<--- Score

59. What are some potential dangers of overlapping activities in any type of process?
<--- Score

60. Major outputs from the development phase are scripts to check hardware and software configurations of environments before deployment
<--- Score

61. What are the phases of the software development process?

<--- Score

62. What is the process for authentication to the System?

<--- Score

63. What different methods are being used to access the system and data?

<--- Score

64. Which data processing operations should be performed at a client workstation and which on the server?

<--- Score

65. What conclusions were drawn from the team's data collection and analysis? How did the team reach these conclusions?

<--- Score

66. Is the performance gap determined?

<--- Score

67. Are there physical and environmental controls that should be in place to protect the system and data?

<--- Score

68. Will this system collect federal data?

<--- Score

69. What are the roles of Contractors in the maintenance process?

<--- Score

70. Does your SDLC include DevOps tools and process?

<--- Score

71. Does the CMM provide explicit support for improving software maintenance processes?

<--- Score

72. What do you mean by the process is repeatable?

<--- Score

73. Do you, as a leader, bounce back quickly from setbacks?

<--- Score

74. Which risk management process can satisfy managements objective for your project?

<--- Score

75. Is the Deliverable the output of a pre-defined System Development Lifecycle (SDLC) process?

<--- Score

76. How can metrics be used to improve the software maintenance process and products?

<--- Score

77. Where is the data coming from to measure compliance?

<--- Score

78. What do you need the system to output?

<--- Score

79. What will drive CSSLP change?
<--- Score

80. What tools were used to generate the list of possible causes?
<--- Score

81. The expectations for validation of work over the internet are fairly clear, but encryption is not. since encryption actually transforms the data, how is this expected to be validated?
<--- Score

82. Databases are cached?
<--- Score

83. What happens when you are told something is in scope only to be told later in the process its not in scope by the other contractor?
<--- Score

84. What did the team gain from developing a sub-process map?
<--- Score

85. What are the revised rough estimates of the financial savings/opportunity for CSSLP improvements?
<--- Score

86. How will elements in the requirements and design that do not make sense or are un-testable be processed?
<--- Score

87. How often will data be collected for measures?

<--- Score

88. How do you implement and manage your work processes to ensure that they meet design requirements?
<--- Score

89. Is the gap/opportunity displayed and communicated in financial terms?
<--- Score

90. Think about some of the processes you undertake within your organization, which do you own?
<--- Score

91. How do you turn risk management in the SDLC into a process?
<--- Score

92. What quality tools were used to get through the analyze phase?
<--- Score

93. With this new, "full-stack" approach to software delivery comes new opportunity for delay. DevOps was developed as a reaction to the long lead times required for infrastructure provisioning and integration with bureaucracy-laden ITIL processes. But what are these new sources of delay in the software development lifecycle?
<--- Score

94. What are the overall risks to the project with an emphasis on the testing process?
<--- Score

95. Do we measure the responsiveness and quality provided to our stakeholders. Have commitments been met, software deployed, response times honored, processes documented, training completed?
<--- Score

96. How do you identify specific CSSLP investment opportunities and emerging trends?
<--- Score

97. What security controls are in place currently, to prevent the unauthorized modification of the data?
<--- Score

98. What happens when you are told something is in scope only to be told later in the process its not in scope?
<--- Score

99. Think about the functions involved in your CSSLP project, what processes flow from these functions?
<--- Score

100. Did any value-added analysis or 'lean thinking' take place to identify some of the gaps shown on the 'as is' process map?
<--- Score

101. An organizationally feasible system request is one that considers the mission, goals and objectives of the organization. Key questions are: is the CSSLP solution request practical and will it solve a problem or take advantage of an opportunity to achieve company goals?

<--- Score

102. What other organizational variables, such as reward systems or communication systems, affect the performance of this CSSLP process?
<--- Score

103. What are your current levels and trends in key measures or indicators of CSSLP product and process performance that are important to and directly serve your customers? How do these results compare with the performance of your competitors and other organizations with similar offerings?
<--- Score

104. A compounding model resolution with available relevant data can often provide insight towards a solution methodology; which CSSLP models, tools and techniques are necessary?
<--- Score

105. What system administrator will have access to the systems and data?
<--- Score

106. Has CMM changes of processes meant any changes to the maintenance work positive or negative?
<--- Score

107. Has the data for the system been classified by the owner?
<--- Score

108. Are records identified that support the business process?

<--- Score

109. How do you test data integrity?
<--- Score

**110. Are the application developers involved
during the initial design and throughout the SDLC
process?**
<--- Score

111. Does it pass an evaluation process?
<--- Score

**112. How do you recognize the opportunities for
reuse?**
<--- Score

**113. What review processes are implemented
to ensure that nonfunctional requirements are
unambiguous, traceable, and testable throughout
the entire SDLC?**
<--- Score

114. What were the financial benefits resulting from
any 'ground fruit or low-hanging fruit' (quick fixes)?
<--- Score

115. What are your best practices for minimizing
CSSLP project risk, while demonstrating incremental
value and quick wins throughout the CSSLP project
lifecycle?
<--- Score

**116. Will your organization share the data for the
system with other entities?**
<--- Score

117. What is the cost of poor quality as supported by the team's analysis?
<--- Score

118. What are the procedures that must be defined for each software project to ensure that a sound SCM process is implemented?
<--- Score

119. Do you need to store raw unmodified log data?
<--- Score

120. What are your CSSLP processes?
<--- Score

121. If data for the system is to be shared with other entities, will your organization implement data exchange agreements with the entities?
<--- Score

122. List any special requirements of system administrators and database administrators who may have access to this system?
<--- Score

123. What data do you make available on servers?
<--- Score

124. Do your employees have the opportunity to do what they do best everyday?
<--- Score

Add up total points for this section:
_ _ _ _ _ = Total points for this section

Divided by: _____ (number of
statements answered) = _____
Average score for this section

Transfer your score to the CSSLP
Index at the beginning of the Self-
Assessment.

CRITERION #5: IMPROVE:

INTENT: Develop a practical solution. Innovate, establish and test the solution and to measure the results.

In my belief, the answer to this question is clearly defined:

5 Strongly Agree

4 Agree

3 Neutral

2 Disagree

1 Strongly Disagree

1. Which SDLC results in the highest degree of user participation?
<--- Score

2. How does the solution remove the key sources of issues discovered in the analyze phase?
<--- Score

3. What are your current levels and trends in key

measures or indicators of workforce and leader development?

<--- Score

4. Risk factors: what are the characteristics of CSSLP that make it risky?

<--- Score

5. Is the implementation plan designed?

<--- Score

6. Why are software developers so productive in the presence of technical and organizational constraints?

<--- Score

7. At what point will vulnerability assessments be performed once the system is put into production (e.g., ongoing risk management after implementation)?

<--- Score

8. Does it avoid poorly executed software handoffs between development, testing, and operations?

<--- Score

9. Were any criteria developed to assist the team in testing and evaluating potential solutions?

<--- Score

10. Who participates in the system development life cycle?

<--- Score

11. Is software assurance considered in all phases of development?

<--- Score

12. What is the ratio between developers and testers?
<--- Score

13. Whats the ratio between developers and testers?
<--- Score

14. What are the activities that take place in the conceptual design phase of the systems development life cycle (SDLC)?
<--- Score

15. So who oversees implementation of the CMDB tasks during software development and/or maintenance?
<--- Score

16. Is the optimal solution selected based on testing and analysis?
<--- Score

17. What metrics are used in your organization for software development?
<--- Score

18. Do you have developers who possess software security related certifications (e.g., the SANS secure coding certifications)?
<--- Score

19. Will development teams outside IT Services work on ESB SDLC environments?
<--- Score

20. What is the software development lifecycle?
<--- Score

21. What is the team's contingency plan for potential problems occurring in implementation?
<--- Score

22. How significant is the improvement in the eyes of the end user?
<--- Score

23. Is the cloud service a Software Development and/or Deployment Platform?
<--- Score

24. How do you keep improving CSSLP?
<--- Score

25. What error proofing will be done to address some of the discrepancies observed in the 'as is' process?
<--- Score

26. How do you find, understand and document the security development needs in the SDLC?
<--- Score

27. How can prototyping help you develop a successful system?
<--- Score

28. What went well, what should change, what can improve?
<--- Score

29. What is CSSLP's impact on utilizing the best

solution(s)?

<--- Score

30. Who controls the risk?

<--- Score

31. How many risk response types are available for a negative risk event in projects?

<--- Score

32. What is the difference between user documentation and user manual?

<--- Score

33. Does the documentation explain how to install, configure, and/or use it securely?

<--- Score

34. Is your organization Records Officer signature on the system design document?

<--- Score

35. What are guidelines for system development?

<--- Score

36. Is pilot data collected and analyzed?

<--- Score

37. Is there a documented procedure in place for traceability?

<--- Score

38. Is delivery of demonstrably secure software a contractual requirement for third-party developed software?

<--- Score

39. How can the systems development life cycle help you implement a new system?
<--- Score

40. At what point will vulnerability assessments be performed once CSSLP is put into production (e.g., ongoing Risk Management after implementation)?
<--- Score

41. Are all records management requirements incorporated into the system design document?
<--- Score

42. Was a pilot designed for the proposed solution(s)?
<--- Score

43. What are the implications of the one critical CSSLP decision 10 minutes, 10 months, and 10 years from now?
<--- Score

44. What is the time table for standing up your MDM solution?
<--- Score

45. Is it important to limit developers access to this systems source code?
<--- Score

46. What are the benefits and challenges of user involvement in product development?
<--- Score

47. Who controls key decisions that will be made?
<--- Score

48. How can application lifecycle management be applied to a global software development context?

<--- Score

49. Usability and CMMI: Does a higher maturity level in product development mean better usability?

<--- Score

50. Are the best solutions selected?

<--- Score

51. What are new sources of delay in the software development lifecycle?

<--- Score

52. Is your organization Records Officer signature on the requirements document?

<--- Score

53. Who will be using the results of the measurement activities?

<--- Score

54. Will you build the application in-house or purchase a solution from an external vendor?

<--- Score

55. How is software risk managed?

<--- Score

56. Has the development team gathered the latest information about security threats and vulnerabilities in the technology and the target

operating environments for the component, product, or solution?

<--- Score

57. Is a solution implementation plan established, including schedule/work breakdown structure, resources, risk management plan, cost/budget, and control plan?

<--- Score

58. Do you combine technical expertise with business knowledge and CSSLP Key topics include lifecycles, development approaches, requirements and how to make a business case?

<--- Score

59. How do you improve CSSLP service perception, and satisfaction?

<--- Score

60. What type of risk response have you elected to use in which instance?

<--- Score

61. Can Distributed Software Development Be Agile?

<--- Score

62. What training/documentation is available for software installation and maintenance?

<--- Score

63. How did the team generate the list of possible solutions?

<--- Score

64. What improvements have been achieved?
<--- Score

65. The organization is going for CMM level 3 accreditation, which changes will improve the daily work in quality and/or efficiency?
<--- Score

66. What exactly is the nature of the risk?
<--- Score

67. How will you know that a change is an improvement?
<--- Score

68. What are the three types of tests performed by system developers?
<--- Score

69. What can you do to improve?
<--- Score

70. What models are used in software development?
<--- Score

71. How does the team improve its work?
<--- Score

72. Is a contingency plan established?
<--- Score

73. How could the architecture description be improved to be more useful during the development and maintenance phases?
<--- Score

74. Who will be responsible for documenting the CSSLP requirements in detail?
<--- Score

75. Evaluate your ideas about project management - do they support or undermine risk management?
<--- Score

76. Why do you need Software Development Life Cycle?
<--- Score

77. Which aspects of the application can be tested early in the development cycle?
<--- Score

78. Explorations of the frontiers of CSSLP will help you build influence, improve CSSLP, optimize decision making, and sustain change, what is your approach?
<--- Score

79. Is there a small-scale pilot for proposed improvement(s)? What conclusions were drawn from the outcomes of a pilot?
<--- Score

80. Does the project require development of new application code or modification of existing code?
<--- Score

81. What is the implementation plan?
<--- Score

82. What are the essential development tools for

product development and deployment?
<--- Score

83. How do you avoid poorly executed software handoffs between development, testing, and operations?
<--- Score

84. Do you have a formal, documented SDLC?
<--- Score

85. Do you agree that the definitions reflect typical current new software development items and the associated guidance is reasonable?
<--- Score

86. How does a risk assessment fit into the SDLC?
<--- Score

87. How can skill-level changes improve CSSLP?
<--- Score

88. Why improve in the first place?
<--- Score

89. What resources are required for the improvement efforts?
<--- Score

90. How do you measure improved CSSLP service perception, and satisfaction?
<--- Score

91. For decision problems, how do you develop a decision statement?
<--- Score

92. Do you cover the five essential competencies: Communication, Collaboration,Innovation, Adaptability, and Leadership that improve an organization's ability to leverage the new CSSLP in a volatile global economy?
<--- Score

93. How will you know that you have improved?
<--- Score

94. Is the solution technically practical?
<--- Score

95. How will the group know that the solution worked?
<--- Score

96. What to do with the results or outcomes of measurements?
<--- Score

97. What type of risk response have you elected to use in each instance?
<--- Score

98. Are there any constraints (technical, political, cultural, or otherwise) that would inhibit certain solutions?
<--- Score

99. What types of measures are appropriate for understanding software productivity?
<--- Score

100. Who makes risk decisions?

<--- Score

101. Can the solution be designed and implemented within an acceptable time period?
<--- Score

102. Who owns the residual risk attributable to exploitable software?
<--- Score

103. What tools were used to evaluate the potential solutions?
<--- Score

104. How do you improve it?
<--- Score

105. Is this a document review, design review, or code review?
<--- Score

106. How will the team or the process owner(s) monitor the implementation plan to see that it is working as intended?
<--- Score

107. What needs improvement? Why?
<--- Score

108. Are systems and rules for the development of software established and changes to systems within the development lifecycle formally controlled?
<--- Score

109. How have you developed staff capabilities

to handle the development, implementation, and maintenance of systems?

<--- Score

110. Do you have sufficient training material & documentation?

<--- Score

111. What actually has to improve and by how much?

<--- Score

112. Is there a cost/benefit analysis of optimal solution(s)?

<--- Score

113. What observable behavior might put your organization at risk?

<--- Score

114. What tools were used to tap into the creativity and encourage 'outside the box' thinking?

<--- Score

115. What does the 'should be' process map/design look like?

<--- Score

116. What is the role of documentation in QA?

<--- Score

117. When are defects identified in the software development lifecycle?

<--- Score

118. Do you understand what may be needed for back-office software maintenance?

<--- Score

119. How will you measure the results?
<--- Score

120. How do you link measurement and risk?
<--- Score

121. What lessons, if any, from a pilot were incorporated into the design of the full-scale solution?
<--- Score

122. What are the five steps in the systems development life cycle (SDLC)?
<--- Score

123. What communications are necessary to support the implementation of the solution?
<--- Score

124. Have you been involved in the development of this application?
<--- Score

125. What tools were most useful during the improve phase?
<--- Score

126. At what points will risk assessments be performed throughout the SDLC?
<--- Score

127. Is the core financial system a commercially available product, subject to regular maintenance based on vendor-developed and scheduled software releases?

<--- Score

128. What attendant changes will need to be made to ensure that the solution is successful?
<--- Score

129. How can you improve performance?
<--- Score

130. Are you assessing CSSLP and risk?
<--- Score

131. Is there a high likelihood that any recommendations will achieve their intended results?
<--- Score

132. Describe the design of the pilot and what tests were conducted, if any?
<--- Score

133. How can you improve CSSLP?
<--- Score

134. Who inherits the residual risk?
<--- Score

135. Does your company develop security measurement objectives for phases of the SDLC?
<--- Score

136. What were the underlying assumptions on the cost-benefit analysis?
<--- Score

137. Does scm apply to the source code and documentation?

<--- Score

Add up total points for this section:
_____ = Total points for this section

Divided by: _____ (number of
statements answered) = _____
Average score for this section

Transfer your score to the CSSLP
Index at the beginning of the Self-
Assessment.

CRITERION #6: CONTROL:

INTENT: Implement the practical solution. Maintain the performance and correct possible complications.

In my belief, the answer to this question is clearly defined:

5 Strongly Agree

4 Agree

3 Neutral

2 Disagree

1 Strongly Disagree

1. Is there a transfer of ownership and knowledge to process owner and process team tasked with the responsibilities.
<--- Score

2. What should you measure to verify efficiency gains?
<--- Score

3. How will the day-to-day responsibilities for

monitoring and continual improvement be transferred from the improvement team to the process owner?
<--- Score

4. What should the next improvement project be that is related to CSSLP?
<--- Score

5. How do you plan and develop for maintenance?
<--- Score

6. How does the product fit into existing systems, and conform to department and company standards?
<--- Score

7. Does your organizations five year IT capital plan address information security and privacy as related to this system?
<--- Score

8. How do your controls stack up?
<--- Score

9. How will the software maintenance process be monitored?
<--- Score

10. Does CSSLP appropriately measure and monitor risk?
<--- Score

11. Has your organization adopted the Systems Development Life Cycle (SDLC) as a standard for benchmarking progress on a project?

<--- Score

12. Is a response plan established and deployed?
<--- Score

13. What impact does Business Planning Estimate (BPE) have on the timing of the projects?
<--- Score

14. What key inputs and outputs are being measured on an ongoing basis?
<--- Score

15. Does a troubleshooting guide exist or is it needed?
<--- Score

16. Is the software process followed and software engineering standards applied?
<--- Score

17. Project Cost- Is the CMM product a standard, affordable, off-the-shelf software package that requires minimal or no customization by the Vendor?
<--- Score

18. What is the difference between a test plan and a test scenario?
<--- Score

19. You may have created your quality measures at a time when you lacked resources, technology wasn't up to the required standard, or low service levels were the industry norm. Have those circumstances changed?
<--- Score

20. How do you plan for maintenance?
<--- Score

21. Is new knowledge gained imbedded in the response plan?
<--- Score

22. What security measurement practices and data does your organization use to assist product planning?
<--- Score

23. Does the CSSLP performance meet the customer's requirements?
<--- Score

24. What secure development standards and/or guidelines are provided to developers?
<--- Score

25. Do you have diagrams of the entire system for completeness and consistency for quality control, diagnostic and maintenance purposes?
<--- Score

26. What are the known security controls?
<--- Score

27. Is system secure against external attack ?
<--- Score

28. Does the system use role based access control?
<--- Score

29. What are the different plans/levels of support

and maintenance that a user can subscribe to?

<--- Score

30. Where do you plan to extend this IT capability or innovation?

<--- Score

31. What is the purpose of a test plan?

<--- Score

32. What other areas of the group might benefit from the CSSLP team's improvements, knowledge, and learning?

<--- Score

33. Is the code bug-free, structured properly, and written in accordance with design standards?

<--- Score

34. What is the best design framework for CSSLP organization now that, in a post industrial-age if the top-down, command and control model is no longer relevant?

<--- Score

35. Are suggested corrective/restorative actions indicated on the response plan for known causes to problems that might surface?

<--- Score

36. Who is the CSSLP process owner?

<--- Score

37. How will input, process, and output variables be checked to detect for sub-optimal conditions?

<--- Score

38. Are documented procedures clear and easy to follow for the operators?
<--- Score

39. How will new or emerging customer needs/ requirements be checked/communicated to orient the process toward meeting the new specifications and continually reducing variation?
<--- Score

40. Is a response plan in place for when the input, process, or output measures indicate an 'out-of-control' condition?
<--- Score

41. What other systems, operations, processes, and infrastructures (hiring practices, staffing, training, incentives/rewards, metrics/dashboards/scorecards, etc.) need updates, additions, changes, or deletions in order to facilitate knowledge transfer and improvements?
<--- Score

42. Project Cos: tls the CMMS product a standard, affordable, off-the-shelf software package that requires minimal or no customization by the Vendor?
<--- Score

43. How will the process owner and team be able to hold the gains?
<--- Score

44. What are the basic elements of a maintenance plan ?

<--- Score

45. Is reporting being used or needed?
<--- Score

46. Do you monitor the effectiveness of your CSSLP activities?
<--- Score

47. How will report readings be checked to effectively monitor performance?
<--- Score

48. Are operating procedures consistent?
<--- Score

49. Does job training on the documented procedures need to be part of the process team's education and training?
<--- Score

50. How will the process owner verify improvement in present and future sigma levels, process capabilities?
<--- Score

51. Assess the adequacy of maintenance project management standards, methodologies, and practices. Does your organization have adequate maintenance standards and controls?
<--- Score

52. Planning and preparing for deployment are managed
<--- Score

53. What are the critical parameters to watch?

<--- Score

54. Communication plan; who needs to get what information when?
<--- Score

55. What is the software project test plan?
<--- Score

56. Is there a documented and implemented monitoring plan?
<--- Score

57. In which type of access control do user ID and password system come under?
<--- Score

58. Does your organizations IT capital plan address information security and privacy as related to this system?
<--- Score

59. Who Has Control?
<--- Score

60. Who will be in control?
<--- Score

61. How do you encourage people to take control and responsibility?
<--- Score

62. Is there a recommended audit plan for routine surveillance inspections of CSSLP's gains?
<--- Score

63. How do you select, collect, align, and integrate CSSLP data and information for tracking daily operations and overall organizational performance, including progress relative to strategic objectives and action plans?
<--- Score

64. Implementation Planning: is a pilot needed to test the changes before a full roll out occurs?
<--- Score

65. Where do ideas that reach policy makers and planners as proposals for CSSLP strengthening and reform actually originate?
<--- Score

66. What do you stand for--and what are you against?
<--- Score

67. How will IoT edge devices be monitored, managed and updated?
<--- Score

68. Is there a control plan in place for sustaining improvements (short and long-term)?
<--- Score

69. Are pertinent alerts monitored, analyzed and distributed to appropriate personnel?
<--- Score

70. What is the planning phase?
<--- Score

71. What quality tools were useful in the control phase?

<--- Score

72. What are you attempting to measure/monitor?
<--- Score

73. Are the planned controls in place?
<--- Score

74. What do you want to protect against?
<--- Score

75. Who can approve the process as complete and allow the project to proceed to the next level (depending on the level of the plan)?
<--- Score

76. Has the improved process and its steps been standardized?
<--- Score

77. Does the response plan contain a definite closed loop continual improvement scheme (e.g., plan-do-check-act)?
<--- Score

78. Will any special training be provided for results interpretation?
<--- Score

79. Is there documentation that will support the successful operation of the improvement?
<--- Score

80. How does the product fit into existing systems, and conform to department and organization standards?

<--- Score

81. What is to be delivered as part of this plan?
<--- Score

82. How can you best use all of your knowledge repositories to enhance learning and sharing?
<--- Score

83. What is the purpose of your test plan?
<--- Score

84. What are the basic elements of a maintenance plan?
<--- Score

85. Have you developed a plan for implementation of the concept of operations?
<--- Score

86. Do software plans address development tools in terms of availability, support, maintenance, and training?
<--- Score

87. Who controls critical resources?
<--- Score

88. Is knowledge gained on process shared and institutionalized?
<--- Score

89. Are you learning proper mitigation tactics?
<--- Score

90. Is there a standardized process?

<--- Score

91. What is the recommended frequency of auditing?
<--- Score

92. Are new process steps, standards, and documentation ingrained into normal operations?
<--- Score

93. Are the planned controls working?
<--- Score

94. What is the control/monitoring plan?
<--- Score

95. Communication plan who needs to get what information when?
<--- Score

96. How might the group capture best practices and lessons learned so as to leverage improvements?
<--- Score

97. Are there documented procedures?
<--- Score

98. Should business employees learn how to design databases according to the SDLC process?
<--- Score

99. Is there a test plan in place and are tools available to perform security testing?
<--- Score

100. Our project management standards - do they support or undermine Risk Management?

<--- Score

101. Have new or revised work instructions resulted?
<--- Score

Add up total points for this section:
_ _ _ _ _ = Total points for this section

Divided by: _ _ _ _ _ _ (number of
statements answered) = _ _ _ _ _ _
Average score for this section

Transfer your score to the CSSLP
Index at the beginning of the Self-
Assessment.

CRITERION #7: SUSTAIN:

INTENT: Retain the benefits.

In my belief, the answer to this question is clearly defined:

5 Strongly Agree

4 Agree

3 Neutral

2 Disagree

1 Strongly Disagree

1. What is the difference between alpha and beta testing?
<--- Score

2. How do you create buy-in?
<--- Score

3. What is the difference between bug and defect?
<--- Score

4. How can you be effective and efficient, when

you do black box testing of ecommerce web sites?

<--- Score

5. What is the difference between a software fault and software failure?

<--- Score

6. Has software been reviewed to confirm that it does not infringe upon any copyright or patent?

<--- Score

7. What is the difference between volume testing and load testing?

<--- Score

8. Transfer, Deployment and retirement are managed

<--- Score

9. What can go wrong?

<--- Score

10. Is there any specific software that you use?

<--- Score

11. What are the quality assurance activities of the maintenance team?

<--- Score

12. When do you choose automated testing?

<--- Score

13. Source Code. Is it a reasonable request to ask for source code should the software vendor cease operations?

<--- Score

14. Why white box testing?
<--- Score

15. In a project to restructure CSSLP outcomes, which stakeholders would you involve?
<--- Score

16. Who will determine interim and final deadlines?
<--- Score

17. What is your black box testing?
<--- Score

18. Have maintenance procedures been established for storage and distribution?
<--- Score

19. What IT systems do you have in your organization?
<--- Score

20. Who are the key stakeholders?
<--- Score

21. Is the system designed correctly?
<--- Score

22. What is the relationship between software testing and software maintenance ?
<--- Score

23. What is the estimated value of the project?
<--- Score

24. Why should you use static testing techniques?

<--- Score

25. Do back-up policies address all critical hardware and software, including personnel workstations?
<--- Score

26. What are the key contributors to software maintenance complexity?
<--- Score

27. Verification: am I building the product right?
<--- Score

28. Who will build the system?
<--- Score

29. What is your strategy for addressing the change to programming models for your organization?
<--- Score

30. Are any compiler warnings disabled in code being delivered?
<--- Score

31. What is the difference between system testing and integration testing?
<--- Score

32. Who does testing and in what order?
<--- Score

33. What is the difference between efficient and effective?
<--- Score

34. Single Loss Expectancy (SLE) represents an organizations loss from a single threat. Which formulas best describes the Single Loss Expectancy (SLE) for your organization?
<--- Score

35. How do you foster innovation?
<--- Score

36. Who has access?
<--- Score

37. What are good and easy practices for frequent web deployments?
<--- Score

38. How will you insure seamless interoperability of CSSLP moving forward?
<--- Score

39. How will the product be deployed to the production environment?
<--- Score

40. Have training materials been completed for Operations, Support and end-users?
<--- Score

41. What is the difference between version and release?
<--- Score

42. What are the Exit criteria?
<--- Score

43. Who is on the team?
<--- Score

44. Does the software diagnose itself prior to and perhaps during operations?
<--- Score

45. What kinds of tests could easily cover multiple functionalities?
<--- Score

46. Validation: are you building the right product?
<--- Score

47. Who uses the system in what roles?
<--- Score

48. What are the parameters of peer reviews?
<--- Score

49. How will this new system be installed?
<--- Score

50. Validation: am I building the right product?
<--- Score

51. What metrics will be collected?
<--- Score

52. Who is responsible for User Acceptance Testing (UAT) for maintenance?
<--- Score

53. Think of your CSSLP project, what are the main functions?
<--- Score

54. What is the delivery model for your MDM platform (i.e. on premise, hosted, hybrid, or other)?
<--- Score

55. What is the type and duration of the license model?
<--- Score

56. How will periodic review of users rights and access be performed and by who?
<--- Score

57. Is it necessary to have specifications on scanning or scalability?
<--- Score

58. Where should you protect them (What areas of the application)?
<--- Score

59. How is the software architecture designed?
<--- Score

60. What are the uses of the system?
<--- Score

61. When should information security considerations factor into the SDLC?
<--- Score

62. How do you decide how much to remunerate an employee?
<--- Score

63. How do you determine when the system is ready for delivery?

<--- Score

64. Is there a discount for multi-year contracts?

<--- Score

65. What type of defects lead to security vulnerabilities?

<--- Score

66. Why is it important to have senior management support for a CSSLP project?

<--- Score

67. What are the primary advantages of the traditional SDLC?

<--- Score

68. Are any special tools to be used and what are they?

<--- Score

69. What you want to protect?

<--- Score

70. What black box testing types do you perform?

<--- Score

71. Who do we want your customers to become?

<--- Score

72. Who backs it up?

<--- Score

73. What determines whether or not software is

good?

<--- Score

74. When does security testing occur during the SDLC (e.g., unit level, subsystem, system, certification and accreditation)?

<--- Score

75. Cross-border flow of health information: is privacy by design enough?

<--- Score

76. How will pending maintenance activities be handled?

<--- Score

77. Are there on-going maintenance projects?

<--- Score

78. What are the top challenges?

<--- Score

79. In which SDLC phase is the information system coded, tested, and installed in your organization?

<--- Score

80. Vendor time commitments are these slipping?

<--- Score

81. Does any action affect the confidentially, integrity or availability of the system?

<--- Score

82. What are some of the software Configuration Management tools?

<--- Score

83. What is your disaster recovery testing?
<--- Score

84. Which models, tools and techniques are necessary?
<--- Score

85. What may be the consequences for the performance of an organization if all stakeholders are not consulted regarding CSSLP?
<--- Score

86. Does the CMM framework address unique software maintenance aspects?
<--- Score

87. How will end users be instructed on the new product?
<--- Score

88. What are the types of software maintenance?
<--- Score

89. Is CSSLP realistic, or are you setting yourself up for failure?
<--- Score

90. How the work will be done, who will do it, and how long will it take?
<--- Score

91. Is access to the safety-critical sections of the software limited to authorized and competent people?
<--- Score

92. What features are important?
<--- Score

93. Do you use static testing techniques?
<--- Score

94. Deployment verification is managed
<--- Score

95. What if there is not enough time for thorough testing?
<--- Score

96. Can provisioning software speed up new server deployments?
<--- Score

97. Are any special tools to be used and what are others?
<--- Score

98. Which heuristics increase the applications attack surface?
<--- Score

99. What interfaces are to be established?
<--- Score

100. What metrics are used for bug tracking?
<--- Score

101. Are licensed software components still valid for the intended use?
<--- Score

102. What testing tools do you use?
<--- Score

103. Why are SDLCs important?
<--- Score

104. What trouble can you get into?
<--- Score

105. What are the policies and procedures used to protect sensitive information from unauthorized access?
<--- Score

106. Does your organization have the right skills, infrastructure, sla, sdlc in place?
<--- Score

107. What is the role of the Portfolio Manager and the Program Office during transition?
<--- Score

108. How do you check the security of your application?
<--- Score

109. What is the difference between performance testing and load testing?
<--- Score

110. Staff support end user buy-in, power users -is staff included?
<--- Score

111. How does the CMM treat maintenance?
<--- Score

112. What is your software configuration management?

<--- Score

113. How can you be sure your systems conform to policy?

<--- Score

114. How do you engage the workforce, in addition to satisfying them?

<--- Score

115. Integrity; is it secure ?

<--- Score

116. Ability to activate and update agents either by manual installation or over-the-air installation?

<--- Score

117. In what step in the SDLC do you build the technical architecture?

<--- Score

118. What kinds of authority can software components and other users hold?

<--- Score

119. Anti-virus software running on server?

<--- Score

120. How the software architecture to be designed?

<--- Score

121. Do you have someone on your maintenance

staff with enterprise software implementation experience?

<--- Score

122. Will this be an internal tool, or a public-facing B-to-B application or site?

<--- Score

123. What current security weaknesses may expose the assets to such threats?

<--- Score

124. How does the complexity of a software system affect the maintenance task?

<--- Score

125. Is the software in question original source or a modified version?

<--- Score

126. Who should have access to the source code repository for this system?

<--- Score

127. Is program build testing meant to be equivalent to unit testing?

<--- Score

128. What areas of the business are you going to offer services (and which services) to?

<--- Score

129. How long will it take to change?

<--- Score

130. Why should you carry out white box testing

on a software product?

<--- Score

131. What is the difference between monkey testing and smoke testing?

<--- Score

132. What functions and performances are desired?

<--- Score

133. Technical Feasibility: Whether the project can be carried out with existing system?

<--- Score

134. How can you be a good tester?

<--- Score

135. Are all the attendees well prepared for peer reviews?

<--- Score

136. What is the funding source for this project?

<--- Score

137. Review and closing of a deployment is managed

<--- Score

138. Which aspects of the application are most important to the customer?

<--- Score

139. What is the difference between top down and bottom up design?

<--- Score

140. License Duration. What is the type and duration of the license model?
<--- Score

141. How will you know that the CSSLP project has been successful?
<--- Score

142. Buffers built in?
<--- Score

143. What are the different categories of penetration testing?
<--- Score

144. What is your formula for success in CSSLP ?
<--- Score

145. How do you address the cyber security challenge?
<--- Score

146. What is CMM?
<--- Score

147. What weaknesses in your organizations software could be exploited?
<--- Score

148. If you were responsible for initiating and implementing major changes in your organization, what steps might you take to ensure acceptance of those changes?
<--- Score

149. What if there isnt enough time for thorough testing?
<--- Score

150. Do you have good enough people?
<--- Score

151. Does Senior Management support working in an agile environment?
<--- Score

152. The organization is going for CMM level 3 accreditation, which changes will negatively affect your work in quality and/or efficiency?
<--- Score

153. What is the kind of project structure that would be appropriate for your CSSLP project, should it be formal and complex, or can it be less formal and relatively simple?
<--- Score

154. How can you support a new employee?
<--- Score

155. What is the implementation phase?
<--- Score

156. Does the software utilize a responsive design?
<--- Score

157. Is the customer's hardware up to the job?
<--- Score

158. What are the short and long-term CSSLP goals?

<--- Score

159. How do you conduct peer reviews?
<--- Score

160. How can you be effective and efficient, when you do black box testing?
<--- Score

161. What happens when a new employee joins the organization?
<--- Score

162. What is the timeline for the deployment of this system?
<--- Score

163. How is quality being addressed on the project?
<--- Score

164. What are the customer privacy policies?
<--- Score

165. What is role of the qa engineer?
<--- Score

166. What is the difference between static and dynamic testing?
<--- Score

167. What design constrains exits?
<--- Score

168. What cloud deployment model is best suited for each of your applications?

<--- Score

169. How can it be known when to stop testing?
<--- Score

170. Which project/projects are you currently working on?
<--- Score

171. Ask yourself: how would you do this work if you only had one staff member to do it?
<--- Score

172. Is there a set of guidelines as to who has to do what in SDLC?
<--- Score

173. Is the behavior of the software under test the same with automation as without?
<--- Score

174. How does your organization know when it is time to replace the old information system with a new one ?
<--- Score

175. How is configuration management performed?
<--- Score

176. Who are you protecting the applications from (malicious attack)?
<--- Score

177. What is the relationship between software quality and software maintenance?

<--- Score

178. Is the design and implementation of secure software possible?
<--- Score

179. What is your competitive advantage?
<--- Score

180. How is Configuration Management handled?
<--- Score

181. What new activities were added to the classic SDLC model and what is main contribution to the success of projects?
<--- Score

182. Does this IT capability already exist and does it currently fulfill the capability requested?
<--- Score

183. What software does the vendor support and which versions?
<--- Score

184. What is your organizations Information Security Governance Structure?
<--- Score

185. What are the barriers to increased CSSLP production?
<--- Score

186. What is the overall business strategy?
<--- Score

187. At the time of retirement or rollover of the system, are records preserved, retained, and fully accessible for the full retentions in accordance with appropriate dispositions?

<--- Score

188. What is the difference between bug and defect in software testing?

<--- Score

189. What is the difference between reliability testing and load testing?

<--- Score

190. How will you ensure you get what you expected?

<--- Score

191. Can the pedigree of the software be established?

<--- Score

192. Is the CSSLP organization completing tasks effectively and efficiently?

<--- Score

193. How do you keep records, of what?

<--- Score

194. How will it be verified that the product is built to accommodate load and growth?

<--- Score

195. How does your organization stack up to the industry in software quality and testing?

<--- Score

196. How does the vendor handle software and hardware maintenance, end user support, and maintenance agreements?
<--- Score

197. Does the interface help the user to make few errors and recover easily from them?
<--- Score

198. How do you determine when to acquire new software?
<--- Score

199. In todays market where web architecture and mobile apps are just what one might expect, and multi-site support is becoming more and more common, is there any noticeable difference between an EAM system and a CMMS?
<--- Score

200. What is your role in your current organization if you are a qa engineer?
<--- Score

201. Vendor and organization reliability are they following through on promises?
<--- Score

202. How will logs be reviewed and by who?
<--- Score

203. Will regression testing be based on severity of defects detected?
<--- Score

204. Preparation for build, test and deployment is

managed
<--- Score

205. Is a validation test suite or diagnostic available to validate that the application software is operating correctly and in a secure configuration following installation?
<--- Score

206. What is the outcome of peer review?
<--- Score

207. What role does communication play in the success or failure of a CSSLP project?
<--- Score

208. Time Feasibility: Whether the system can be implemented within the given time constraints?
<--- Score

209. What are the parameters of performance testing?
<--- Score

210. Should any aspects of operations be outsourced?
<--- Score

211. Who will be the custodians and users of the system?
<--- Score

212. Has training been scheduled for support staff, operations, and the client?
<--- Score

213. What is software configuration management in your organization?

<--- Score

214. What is the purpose of your test strategy?

<--- Score

215. Can any of the software (and software team) be reused?

<--- Score

216. What type of license(s) are available for the open source software?

<--- Score

217. Should you install the program on a server or on a workstation?

<--- Score

218. Does the maintenance work include only defects or does it also include system enhancements?

<--- Score

219. What is the client software?

<--- Score

220. Have there been any significant changes to hardware or software?

<--- Score

221. What is the number and severity of defects located?

<--- Score

222. Can your software be accessed via Windows

PCs and Apple Mac computers?

<--- Score

223. How do auditors observe?

<--- Score

224. What are the software configuration management tools?

<--- Score

225. Ongoing maintenance: How will your organization provide for ongoing operations and maintenance of the system?

<--- Score

226. Who are the end users for the system?

<--- Score

227. If the path forward waits until a new generation of devices essentially replaces an old generation of devices which could be somewhere between 5 and 15 years, what does the path forward look like for the legacy devices and their software maintenance?

<--- Score

228. What is the role of the test engineer?

<--- Score

229. Who will be the designated owner of the proposed system (system)?

<--- Score

230. What are the details of system design, configuration, and integration?

<--- Score

231. What is the objective of regression testing?
<--- Score

232. What is the responsibility of a new employee?
<--- Score

233. What types of review meetings do you have?
<--- Score

234. Do you address information security and privacy as related to this system?
<--- Score

235. Who is responsible for on-line help?
<--- Score

236. What are the customer confidentiality policies?
<--- Score

237. What metrics can be used for bug tracking?
<--- Score

238. How do you know what the objectives and expected outcomes should be for Maintenance?
<--- Score

239. Are upgrades included as part of the software maintenance pricing?
<--- Score

240. When indexing into a string, are the limits of the string off by-one errors in indexing operations or in subscript references to arrays?
<--- Score

241. How can you deploy it?

<--- Score

242. What software applications are you protecting?

<--- Score

243. How long have you been working on maintenance with the current application?

<--- Score

244. What is the role of the systems approach in the SDLC?

<--- Score

245. What metrics are used for test report generation?

<--- Score

246. How can you incorporate support to ensure safe and effective use of CSSLP into the services that you provide?

<--- Score

247. Do you know each assets relationship to its use, deployment, records, and listings within a product catalog. What assets are users requesting?

<--- Score

248. How do you manage CSSLP Knowledge Management (KM)?

<--- Score

249. Software cannot be released for use until validation has been completed?

<--- Score

250. What is disaster recovery testing?
<--- Score

251. What will the product do/how will it work?
<--- Score

252. How well can you use the software as it is?
<--- Score

253. How does the CMM map to the consensus-based objectives and expected outcomes for maintenance?
<--- Score

254. What are the agents or scripts executing on servers of hosted applications?
<--- Score

255. What is the role of the accountant in the SDLC?
<--- Score

256. Does functional testing cover all functions of the program?
<--- Score

257. If you do not follow, then how to lead?
<--- Score

258. What is the difference between stress testing and load testing?
<--- Score

259. What levels of regression testing will be done

and how much at each test level?
<--- Score

260. What s the relationship between program size and the number of people involved?
<--- Score

261. What attacks can exploit which weaknesses?
<--- Score

262. What is the role of the QA engineer?
<--- Score

263. What are some reasons to create or modify an information system?
<--- Score

264. Maintenance – Do you keep all licenses under active maintenance, or at least consistent per each infrastructure element (server, etc.), such as Oracle Support, IBM S&S, Microsoft SA?
<--- Score

265. What do you want to accomplish with this system?
<--- Score

266. Is there room for UX?
<--- Score

267. What are the challenges?
<--- Score

268. What is a request for system services?
<--- Score

269. Should users be involved in defining objectives of the software product?
<--- Score

270. Does your software provide role- and group-based security options that allow business users to securely create and publish their work?
<--- Score

271. Are you / should you be revolutionary or evolutionary?
<--- Score

272. How do you perform integration testing?
<--- Score

273. What testing approaches do you use?
<--- Score

274. Off-by-one errors in indexing or subscripting operations?
<--- Score

275. Verification: are you building the product right?
<--- Score

276. Which aspects of similar/related previous projects had large maintenance expenses?
<--- Score

277. What is the difference between build and release?
<--- Score

278. How can virtualization help us ?

<--- Score

279. Which formulas best describes the Single Loss Expectancy (SLE)?
<--- Score

280. Why an object orientation?
<--- Score

281. What is the difference between verification and validation?
<--- Score

282. What does DevOps look like - across the SDLC?
<--- Score

283. At the time of retirement or rollover of the system, are temporary records destroyed in accordance with appropriate dispositions?
<--- Score

284. How will it affect the IT operations environment?
<--- Score

285. What is the difference between software bug and software defect?
<--- Score

286. Is it correct and operating as you thought it should?
<--- Score

287. What is the maximum number of apps the library can support?

<--- Score

288. Which is least likely to be an accountant s role in the SDLC?
<--- Score

289. Does it have all the basic elements?
<--- Score

Add up total points for this section:
_____ = Total points for this section

Divided by: _____ (number of statements answered) = _____
Average score for this section

Transfer your score to the CSSLP Index at the beginning of the Self-Assessment.

CSSLP and Managing Projects, Criteria for Project Managers:

1.0 Initiating Process Group: CSSLP

1. Specific - is the objective clear in terms of what, how, when, and where the situation will be changed?

2. Have you evaluated the teams performance and asked for feedback?

3. What areas does the group agree are the biggest success on the CSSLP project?

4. What areas were overlooked on this CSSLP project?

5. Information sharing?

6. How can you make your needs known?

7. Based on your CSSLP project communication management plan, what worked well?

8. When are the deliverables to be generated in each phase?

9. Are you certain deliverables are properly completed and meet quality standards?

10. What are the tools and techniques to be used in each phase?

11. What is the NEXT thing to do?

12. At which cmmi level are software processes documented, standardized, and integrated into a standard to-be practiced process for your organization?

13. What input will you be required to provide the CSSLP project team?

14. What must be done?

15. Establishment of pm office?

16. Which six sigma dmaic phase focuses on why and how defects and errors occur?

17. Are the changes in your CSSLP project being formally requested, analyzed, and approved by the appropriate decision makers?

18. Where must it be done?

19. Are you properly tracking the progress of the CSSLP project and communicating the status to stakeholders?

20. During which stage of Risk planning are risks prioritized based on probability and impact?

1.1 Project Charter: CSSLP

21. Pop quiz – which are the same inputs as in the CSSLP project charter?

22. What are the assigned resources?

23. How much?

24. Does the CSSLP project need to consider any special capacity or capability issues?

25. Market – identify products market, including whether it is outside of the objective: what is the purpose of the program or CSSLP project?

26. What are you striving to accomplish (measurable goal(s))?

27. Assumptions and constraints: what assumptions were made in defining the CSSLP project?

28. Will this replace an existing product?

29. Whose input and support will this CSSLP project require?

30. Is it an improvement over existing products?

31. What is the business need?

32. Where does all this information come from?

33. Are there special technology requirements?

34. How will you know that a change is an improvement?

35. Why Outsource?

36. What outcome, in measureable terms, are you hoping to accomplish?

37. Why executive support?

38. What is the justification?

39. What are the known stakeholder requirements?

40. Who will take notes, document decisions?

1.2 Stakeholder Register: CSSLP

41. How big is the gap?

42. What are the major CSSLP project milestones requiring communications or providing communications opportunities?

43. What & Why?

44. What is the power of the stakeholder?

45. Who is managing stakeholder engagement?

46. Who are the stakeholders?

47. How will reports be created?

48. How should employers make voices heard?

49. How much influence do they have on the CSSLP project?

50. Who wants to talk about Security?

51. Is your organization ready for change?

52. What opportunities exist to provide communications?

1.3 Stakeholder Analysis Matrix: CSSLP

53. Cashflow, start-up cash-drain?

54. Why do you care?

55. Industry or lifestyle trends?

56. What is the stakeholders power and status in relation to the CSSLP project?

57. What is relationship with the CSSLP project?

58. What is the stakeholders mandate, what is mission?

59. Who are potential allies and opponents?

60. Which conditions out of the control of the management are crucial to contribute for the achievement of the development objective?

61. Effects on core activities, distraction?

62. Market developments?

63. Are there two or three that rise to the top, and a couple that are sliding to the bottom?

64. Morale, commitment, leadership?

65. What is your Advocacy Strategy?

66. Tactics: eg, surprise, major contracts?

67. Contributions to policy and practice?

68. Partnership opportunities/synergies?

69. Do any safeguard policies apply to the CSSLP project?

70. Beneficiaries; who are the potential beneficiaries?

71. Are they likely to influence the success or failure of your CSSLP project?

72. New USPs?

2.0 Planning Process Group: CSSLP

73. How well will the chosen processes produce the expected results?

74. Have operating capacities been created and/or reinforced in partners?

75. How will it affect you?

76. To what extent are the visions and actions of the partners consistent or divergent with regard to the program?

77. If action is called for, what form should it take?

78. What is the difference between the early schedule and late schedule?

79. Are the necessary foundations in place to ensure the sustainability of the results of the CSSLP project?

80. If task x starts two days late, what is the effect on the CSSLP project end date?

81. To what extent are the participating departments coordinating with each other?

82. What should you do next?

83. Will the products created live up to the necessary quality?

84. Are the follow-up indicators relevant and do they

meet the quality needed to measure the outputs and outcomes of the CSSLP project?

85. In which CSSLP project management process group is the detailed CSSLP project budget created?

86. When will the CSSLP project be done?

87. How will users learn how to use the deliverables?

88. Mitigate. what will you do to minimize the impact should a risk event occur?

89. What will you do?

90. Are you just doing busywork to pass the time?

91. To what extent and in what ways are the CSSLP project contributing to progress towards organizational reform?

92. Does the program have follow-up mechanisms (to verify the quality of the products, punctuality of delivery, etc.) to measure progress in the achievement of the envisaged results?

2.1 Project Management Plan: CSSLP

93. What happened during the process that you found interesting?

94. Does the implementation plan have an appropriate division of responsibilities?

95. What did not work so well?

96. How can you best help your organization to develop consistent practices in CSSLP project management planning stages?

97. What goes into your CSSLP project Charter?

98. Who is the sponsor?

99. What are the training needs?

100. When is the CSSLP project management plan created?

101. Are the existing and future without-plan conditions reasonable and appropriate?

102. What are the deliverables?

103. If the CSSLP project is complex or scope is specialized, do you have appropriate and/or qualified staff available to perform the tasks?

104. Why do you manage integration?

105. How do you manage time?

106. What would you do differently what did not work?

107. What should you drop in order to add something new?

108. Are cost risk analysis methods applied to develop contingencies for the estimated total CSSLP project costs?

109. Is there an incremental analysis/cost effectiveness analysis of proposed mitigation features based on an approved method and using an accepted model?

110. Is mitigation authorized or recommended?

2.2 Scope Management Plan: CSSLP

111. What do you need to do to accomplish the goal or goals?

112. Are estimating assumptions and constraints captured?

113. Quality standards - are controls in place to ensure that the work was not only completed and also completed to meet specific standards?

114. Deliverables -are the deliverables tangible and verifiable?

115. What problem is being solved by delivering this CSSLP project?

116. Describe the process for accepting the CSSLP project deliverables. Will the CSSLP project deliverables become accepted in writing?

117. Are the CSSLP project plans updated on a frequent basis?

118. Staffing Requirements?

119. Have all team members been part of identifying risks?

120. Have you identified possible roadblocks?

121. Are changes in scope (deliverable commitments) agreed to by all affected groups & individuals?

122. How relevant is this attribute to this CSSLP project or audit?

123. Is there a set of procedures defining the scope, procedures, and deliverables defining quality control?

124. Are any non-compliance issues that exist due to organizations practices?

125. Is there a requirements change management processes in place?

126. Do you secure formal approval of changes and requirements from stakeholders?

127. Have all necessary approvals been obtained?

128. Are the CSSLP project team members located locally to the users/stakeholders?

129. Assess the expected stability of the scope of this CSSLP project how likely is it to change, how frequently, and by how much?

130. Is there a scope management plan that includes how CSSLP project scope will be defined, developed, monitored, validated and controlled?

2.3 Requirements Management Plan: CSSLP

131. Will the contractors involved take full responsibility?

132. What are you trying to do?

133. How detailed should the CSSLP project get?

134. Did you use declarative statements?

135. In case of software development; Should you have a test for each code module?

136. Who has the authority to reject CSSLP project requirements?

137. How often will the reporting occur?

138. Is stakeholder risk tolerance an important factor for the requirements process in this CSSLP project?

139. What are you counting on?

140. After the requirements are gathered and set forth on the requirements register, theyre little more than a laundry list of items. Some may be duplicates, some might conflict with others and some will be too broad or too vague to understand. Describe how the requirements will be analyzed. Who will perform the analysis?

141. Define the help desk model. who will take full responsibility?

142. Which hardware or software, related to, or as outcome of the CSSLP project is new to your organization?

143. What went wrong?

144. How do you know that you have done this right?

145. Who will approve the requirements (and if multiple approvers, in what order)?

146. Who is responsible for quantifying the CSSLP project requirements?

147. Will the CSSLP project requirements become approved in writing?

148. Is requirements work dependent on any other specific CSSLP project or non-CSSLP project activities (e.g. funding, approvals, procurement)?

149. Did you provide clear and concise specifications?

150. Controlling CSSLP project requirements involves monitoring the status of the CSSLP project requirements and managing changes to the requirements. Who is responsible for monitoring and tracking the CSSLP project requirements?

2.4 Requirements Documentation: CSSLP

151. What are the attributes of a customer?

152. Are all functions required by the customer included?

153. How do you know when a Requirement is accurate enough?

154. What can tools do for us?

155. What is effective documentation?

156. How much does requirements engineering cost?

157. Validity. does the system provide the functions which best support the customers needs?

158. Is the requirement realistically testable?

159. Where do system and software requirements come from, what are sources?

160. Does the system provide the functions which best support the customers needs?

161. Verifiability. can the requirements be checked?

162. Who is interacting with the system?

163. Completeness. are all functions required by the

customer included?

164. Do technical resources exist?

165. Are there legal issues?

166. What are the acceptance criteria?

167. What kind of entity is a problem ?

168. If applicable; are there issues linked with the fact that this is an offshore CSSLP project?

169. How does the proposed CSSLP project contribute to the overall objectives of your organization?

170. How will they be documented / shared?

2.5 Requirements Traceability Matrix: CSSLP

171. How small is small enough?

172. Why use a WBS?

173. Is there a requirements traceability process in place?

174. What are the chronologies, contingencies, consequences, criteria?

175. How will it affect the stakeholders personally in their career?

176. What is the WBS?

177. How do you manage scope?

178. Why do you manage scope?

179. Describe the process for approving requirements so they can be added to the traceability matrix and CSSLP project work can be performed. Will the CSSLP project requirements become approved in writing?

180. Do you have a clear understanding of all subcontracts in place?

181. What percentage of CSSLP projects are producing traceability matrices between requirements and other work products?

182. Will you use a Requirements Traceability Matrix?

2.6 Project Scope Statement: CSSLP

183. Are the input requirements from the team members clearly documented and communicated?

184. Are there specific processes you will use to evaluate and approve/reject changes?

185. Will statistics related to QA be collected, trends analyzed, and problems raised as issues?

186. Is the plan under configuration management?

187. Were potential customers involved early in the planning process?

188. Will tasks be marked complete only after QA has been successfully completed?

189. Have the configuration management functions been assigned?

190. Identify how your team and you will create the CSSLP project scope statement and the work breakdown structure (WBS). Document how you will create the CSSLP project scope statement and WBS, and make sure you answer the following questions: In defining CSSLP project scope and the WBS, will you and your CSSLP project team be using methods defined by your organization, methods defined by the CSSLP project management office (PMO), or other methods?

191. Is there a process (test plans, inspections,

reviews) defined for verifying outputs for each task?

192. Will the risk plan be updated on a regular and frequent basis?

193. Will the risk documents be filed?

194. Is the quality function identified and assigned?

195. Elements that deal with providing the detail?

196. Change management vs. change leadership - what is the difference?

197. CSSLP project lead, team lead, solution architect?

198. Is there a baseline plan against which to measure progress?

199. Is the change control process documented and on file?

200. Will all CSSLP project issues be unconditionally tracked through the issue resolution process?

201. Was planning completed before the CSSLP project was initiated?

202. Has a method and process for requirement tracking been developed?

2.7 Assumption and Constraint Log: CSSLP

203. How can constraints be violated?

204. Do documented requirements exist for all critical components and areas, including technical, business, interfaces, performance, security and conversion requirements?

205. Have CSSLP project management standards and procedures been established and documented?

206. Does the CSSLP project have a formal CSSLP project Plan?

207. Is there a Steering Committee in place?

208. Contradictory information between different documents?

209. Does the system design reflect the requirements?

210. Is the process working, and people are not executing in compliance of the process?

211. Would known impacts serve as impediments?

212. Does a specific action and/or state that is known to violate security policy occur?

213. Is there documentation of system capability requirements, data requirements, environment

requirements, security requirements, and computer and hardware requirements?

214. If it is out of compliance, should the process be amended or should the Plan be amended?

215. What would you gain if you spent time working to improve this process?

216. Model-building: what data-analytic strategies are useful when building proportional-hazards models?

217. Is the amount of effort justified by the anticipated value of forming a new process?

218. Does the document/deliverable meet all requirements (for example, statement of work) specific to this deliverable?

219. Do you know what your customers expectations are regarding this process?

220. What strengths do you have?

221. Does the traceability documentation describe the tool and/or mechanism to be used to capture traceability throughout the life cycle?

222. Are there unnecessary steps that are creating bottlenecks and/or causing people to wait?

2.8 Work Breakdown Structure: CSSLP

223. How much detail?

224. Why is it useful?

225. Is it a change in scope?

226. How many levels?

227. Where does it take place?

228. How far down?

229. Is the work breakdown structure (wbs) defined and is the scope of the CSSLP project clear with assigned deliverable owners?

230. How big is a work-package?

231. When would you develop a Work Breakdown Structure?

232. What is the probability of completing the CSSLP project in less that xx days?

233. When does it have to be done?

234. When do you stop?

235. Who has to do it?

236. What has to be done?

237. Do you need another level?

238. Is it still viable?

239. How will you and your CSSLP project team define the CSSLP projects scope and work breakdown structure?

240. What is the probability that the CSSLP project duration will exceed xx weeks?

241. Can you make it?

242. Why would you develop a Work Breakdown Structure?

2.9 WBS Dictionary: CSSLP

243. What is the goal?

244. Is the work done on a work package level as described in the WBS dictionary?

245. Should you include sub-activities?

246. Authorization to proceed with all authorized work?

247. Do work packages consist of discrete tasks which are adequately described?

248. Evaluate the performance of operating organizations?

249. Are control accounts opened and closed based on the start and completion of work contained therein?

250. Does the scheduling system identify in a timely manner the status of work?

251. Are data elements reconcilable between internal summary reports and reports forwarded to us?

252. Detailed schedules which support control account and work package start and completion dates/events?

253. Are material costs reported within the same period as that in which BCWP is earned for that

material?

254. Is future work which cannot be planned in detail subdivided to the extent practicable for budgeting and scheduling purposes?

255. Are retroactive changes to direct costs and indirect costs prohibited except for the correction of errors and routine accounting adjustments?

256. Are overhead cost budgets established for each organization which has authority to incur overhead costs?

257. Are management actions taken to reduce indirect costs when there are significant adverse variances?

258. Are records maintained to show full accountability for all material purchased for the contract, including the residual inventory?

259. Are data elements summarized through the functional organizational structure for progressively higher levels of management?

2.10 Schedule Management Plan: CSSLP

260. What is the difference between % Complete and % work?

261. Is there an onboarding process in place?

262. Is a payment system in place with proper reviews and approvals?

263. Are tasks tracked by hours?

264. List all schedule constraints here. Must the CSSLP project be complete by a specified date?

265. Were CSSLP project team members involved in detailed estimating and scheduling?

266. Is documentation created for communication with the suppliers and Vendors?

267. Is funded schedule margin reasonable and logically distributed?

268. Is pert / critical path or equivalent methodology being used?

269. Have adequate resources been provided by management to ensure CSSLP project success?

270. Are decisions captured in a decisions log?

271. Are metrics used to evaluate and manage Vendors?

272. Pareto diagrams, statistical sampling, flow charting or trend analysis used quality monitoring?

273. Are internal CSSLP project status meetings held at reasonable intervals?

274. Are the results of quality assurance reviews provided to affected groups & individuals?

275. Has a CSSLP project Communications Plan been developed?

276. Are any non-compliance issues that exist due to your organizations practices communicated to your organization?

277. Has your organization readiness assessment been conducted?

278. Personnel with expertise?

279. Is your organization certified as a broker of the products/supplies?

2.11 Activity List: CSSLP

280. What is the LF and LS for each activity?

281. How can the CSSLP project be displayed graphically to better visualize the activities?

282. Where will it be performed?

283. Who will perform the work?

284. When do the individual activities need to start and finish?

285. What went well?

286. When will the work be performed?

287. What are the critical bottleneck activities?

288. How do you determine the late start (LS) for each activity?

289. Are the required resources available or need to be acquired?

290. How detailed should a CSSLP project get?

291. What went right?

292. What will be performed?

293. Is infrastructure setup part of your CSSLP project?

294. In what sequence?

295. How much slack is available in the CSSLP project?

296. What did not go as well?

297. Can you determine the activity that must finish, before this activity can start?

2.12 Activity Attributes: CSSLP

298. Does your organization of the data change its meaning?

299. Resources to accomplish the work?

300. What is your organizations history in doing similar activities?

301. Resource is assigned to?

302. How difficult will it be to do specific activities on this CSSLP project?

303. Can more resources be added?

304. How difficult will it be to complete specific activities on this CSSLP project?

305. How much activity detail is required?

306. Why?

307. How else could the items be grouped?

308. Is there anything planned that does not need to be here?

309. Which method produces the more accurate cost assignment?

310. What conclusions/generalizations can you draw from this?

311. Would you consider either of corresponding activities an outlier?

312. Where else does it apply?

313. Are the required resources available?

314. Activity: what is Missing?

2.13 Milestone List: CSSLP

315. How late can the activity start?

316. Usps (unique selling points)?

317. Describe the industry you are in and the market growth opportunities. What is the market for your technology, product or service?

318. How late can each activity be finished and started?

319. Level of the Innovation?

320. How late can the activity finish?

321. How will you get the word out to customers?

322. When will the CSSLP project be complete?

323. Vital contracts and partners?

324. Describe your organizations strengths and core competencies. What factors will make your organization succeed?

325. What background experience, skills, and strengths does the team bring to your organization?

326. Do you foresee any technical risks or developmental challenges?

327. Sustainable financial backing?

328. What has been done so far?

329. What specific improvements did you make to the CSSLP project proposal since the previous time?

330. Global influences?

331. What date will the task finish?

332. Competitive advantages?

2.14 Network Diagram: CSSLP

333. Can you calculate the confidence level?

334. What is the lowest cost to complete this CSSLP project in xx weeks?

335. What is the probability of completing the CSSLP project in less that xx days?

336. What to do and When?

337. How difficult will it be to do specific activities on this CSSLP project?

338. Planning: who, how long, what to do?

339. What activities must follow this activity?

340. What controls the start and finish of a job?

341. Review the logical flow of the network diagram. Take a look at which activities you have first and then sequence the activities. Do they make sense?

342. What activity must be completed immediately before this activity can start?

343. What can be done concurrently?

344. Exercise: what is the probability that the CSSLP project duration will exceed xx weeks?

345. What job or jobs could run concurrently?

346. What are the Key Success Factors?

347. What job or jobs follow it?

348. What activities must occur simultaneously with this activity?

349. If the CSSLP project network diagram cannot change and you have extra personnel resources, what is the BEST thing to do?

350. Will crashing x weeks return more in benefits than it costs?

351. What are the Major Administrative Issues?

2.15 Activity Resource Requirements: CSSLP

352. Do you use tools like decomposition and rolling-wave planning to produce the activity list and other outputs?

353. Time for overtime?

354. When does monitoring begin?

355. How do you handle petty cash?

356. How many signatures do you require on a check and does this match what is in your policy and procedures?

357. Are there unresolved issues that need to be addressed?

358. Organizational Applicability?

359. Other support in specific areas?

360. Why do you do that?

361. What are constraints that you might find during the Human Resource Planning process?

362. Which logical relationship does the PDM use most often?

363. Anything else?

364. What is the Work Plan Standard?

2.16 Resource Breakdown Structure: CSSLP

365. Is predictive resource analysis being done?

366. Who delivers the information?

367. Goals for the CSSLP project. What is each stakeholders desired outcome for the CSSLP project?

368. What is each stakeholders desired outcome for the CSSLP project?

369. What is the primary purpose of the human resource plan?

370. Which resource planning tool provides information on resource responsibility and accountability?

371. How difficult will it be to do specific activities on this CSSLP project?

372. How should the information be delivered?

373. Why is this important?

374. What are the requirements for resource data?

375. When do they need the information?

376. Any changes from stakeholders?

377. Why do you do it?

378. How can this help you with team building?

2.17 Activity Duration Estimates: CSSLP

379. Does the case present a realistic scenario?

380. Which is correct?

381. What is the critical path for this CSSLP project and how long is it?

382. Do your results resemble a normal distribution?

383. What is involved in the solicitation process?

384. Did anything besides luck make a difference between success and failure?

385. Why should CSSLP project managers strive to make jobs look easy?

386. What tasks must precede this task?

387. What are two suggestions for ensuring adequate change control on CSSLP projects that involve outside contracts?

388. Which tips for taking the PMP exam do you think would be most helpful for you?

389. How do functionality, system outputs, performance, reliability, and maintainability requirements affect quality planning?

390. How does poking fun at technical professionals communications skills impact the industry and educational programs?

391. When a risk event occurs, is the risk response evaluated and the appropriate response implemented?

392. Account for the make-or-buy process and how to perform the financial calculations involved in the process. What are the main types of contracts if you do decide to outsource?

393. Account for the four frames of organizations. How can they help CSSLP project managers understand your organizational context for CSSLP projects?

394. Write a oneto two-page paper describing your dream team for this CSSLP project. What type of people would you want on your team?

395. What tasks must follow this task?

396. Are time, scope, cost, and quality monitored throughout the CSSLP project?

2.18 Duration Estimating Worksheet: CSSLP

397. How should ongoing costs be monitored to try to keep the CSSLP project within budget?

398. What utility impacts are there?

399. What work will be included in the CSSLP project?

400. Do any colleagues have experience with your organization and/or RFPs?

401. Can the CSSLP project be constructed as planned?

402. What info is needed?

403. Why estimate costs?

404. What is an Average CSSLP project?

405. Small or large CSSLP project?

406. What is cost and CSSLP project cost management?

407. What is next?

408. Is the CSSLP project responsive to community need?

409. Will the CSSLP project collaborate with the local

community and leverage resources?

410. What is your role?

411. Why estimate time and cost?

412. What questions do you have?

413. Does the CSSLP project provide innovative ways for stakeholders to overcome obstacles or deliver better outcomes?

414. How can the CSSLP project be displayed graphically to better visualize the activities?

415. What is the total time required to complete the CSSLP project if no delays occur?

2.19 Project Schedule: CSSLP

416. Did the CSSLP project come in under budget?

417. How much slack is available in the CSSLP project?

418. Are activities connected because logic dictates the order in which others occur?

419. Why or why not?

420. How closely did the initial CSSLP project Schedule compare with the actual schedule?

421. Did the final product meet or exceed user expectations?

422. Meet requirements?

423. How do you use schedules?

424. How do you know that youhave done this right?

425. Why time management?

426. Eliminate unnecessary activities. Are there activities that came from a template or previous CSSLP project that are not applicable on this phase of this CSSLP project?

427. Does the condition or event threaten the CSSLP projects objectives in any ways?

428. Your CSSLP project management plan results

in a CSSLP project schedule that is too long. If the CSSLP project network diagram cannot change and you have extra personnel resources, what is the BEST thing to do?

429. Are there activities that came from a template or previous CSSLP project that are not applicable on this phase of this CSSLP project?

430. What is the purpose of a CSSLP project schedule?

431. Verify that the update is accurate. Are all remaining durations correct?

432. Are procedures defined by which the CSSLP project schedule may be changed?

2.20 Cost Management Plan: CSSLP

433. Exclusions – is there scope to be performed or provided by others?

434. Is it standard practice to formally commit stakeholders to the CSSLP project via agreements?

435. Outside experts?

436. Have reserves been created to address risks?

437. Are mitigation strategies identified?

438. Scope of work – What is the scope of work for each of the planned contracts?

439. Is a stakeholder management plan in place that covers topics?

440. Have the key elements of a coherent CSSLP project management strategy been established?

441. Is the schedule updated on a periodic basis?

442. Similar CSSLP projects?

443. Are vendor contract reports, reviews and visits conducted periodically?

444. Cost variances – how will cost variances be identified and corrected?

445. Why do you manage cost?

2.21 Activity Cost Estimates: CSSLP

446. Can you delete activities or make them inactive?

447. Where can you get activity reports?

448. Are cost subtotals needed?

449. Were escalated issues resolved promptly?

450. Who determines the quality and expertise of contractors?

451. What procedures are put in place regarding bidding and cost comparisons, if any?

452. What are the audit requirements?

453. Measurable - are the targets measurable?

454. When do you enter into PPM?

455. Were the tasks or work products prepared by the consultant useful?

456. What were things that you did well, and could improve, and how?

457. What skill level is required to do the job?

458. What is your organizations history in doing similar tasks?

459. What do you want to know about the stay to

know if costs were inappropriately high or low?

460. What areas were overlooked on this CSSLP project?

461. What makes a good activity description?

462. Is there anything unique in this CSSLP projects scope statement that will affect resources?

463. Does the activity rely on a common set of tools to carry it out?

464. Estimated cost?

2.22 Cost Estimating Worksheet: CSSLP

465. What happens to any remaining funds not used?

466. Value pocket identification & quantification what are value pockets?

467. Can a trend be established from historical performance data on the selected measure and are the criteria for using trend analysis or forecasting methods met?

468. What is the estimated labor cost today based upon this information?

469. Ask: are others positioned to know, are others credible, and will others cooperate?

470. Is the CSSLP project responsive to community need?

471. What costs are to be estimated?

472. What can be included?

473. Will the CSSLP project collaborate with the local community and leverage resources?

474. Identify the timeframe necessary to monitor progress and collect data to determine how the selected measure has changed?

475. What is the purpose of estimating?

476. Does the CSSLP project provide innovative ways for stakeholders to overcome obstacles or deliver better outcomes?

477. Is it feasible to establish a control group arrangement?

478. Who is best positioned to know and assist in identifying corresponding factors?

479. What will others want?

480. What additional CSSLP project(s) could be initiated as a result of this CSSLP project?

481. How will the results be shared and to whom?

2.23 Cost Baseline: CSSLP

482. What is cost and CSSLP project cost management?

483. Verify business objectives. Are others appropriate, and well-articulated?

484. Have you identified skills that are missing from your team?

485. Has the appropriate access to relevant data and analysis capability been granted?

486. Impact to environment?

487. Are there contingencies or conditions related to the acceptance?

488. Eac -estimate at completion, what is the total job expected to cost?

489. Does the suggested change request seem to represent a necessary enhancement to the product?

490. Pcs for your new business. what would the life cycle costs be?

491. Review your risk triggers -have your risks changed?

492. On budget?

493. Will the CSSLP project fail if the change request is

not executed?

494. Have all approved changes to the schedule baseline been identified and impact on the CSSLP project documented?

495. Who will use corresponding metrics ?

496. Does the suggested change request represent a desired enhancement to the products functionality?

497. For what purpose ?

498. Have the resources used by the CSSLP project been reassigned to other units or CSSLP projects?

499. How will cost estimates be used?

500. Is there anything unique in this CSSLP projects scope statement that will affect resources?

501. Are procedures defined by which the cost baseline may be changed?

2.24 Quality Management Plan: CSSLP

502. Is this a Requirement?

503. How does your organization measure customer satisfaction/dissatisfaction?

504. Are there procedures in place to effectively manage interdependencies with other CSSLP projects / systems?

505. Is this process still needed?

506. How does training support what is important to your organization and the individual?

507. How do you decide what information needs to be recorded?

508. What are you trying to accomplish?

509. You know what your customers expectations are regarding this process?

510. List your organizations customer contact standards that employees are expected to maintain. How are corresponding standards measured?

511. Who is responsible for approving the qapp?

512. Meet how often?

513. Were there any deficiencies / issues in prior years self-assessment?

514. How do you field-modify testing procedures?

515. How are corresponding standards measured?

516. Have all stakeholders been identified?

517. Is there a Quality Management Plan?

518. How does your organization ensure the quality, reliability, and user-friendliness of its hardware and software?

519. Were the right locations/samples tested for the right parameters?

2.25 Quality Metrics: CSSLP

520. Subjective quality component: customer satisfaction, how do you measure it?

521. Do the operators focus on determining; is there anything you need to worry about?

522. How exactly do you define when differences exist?

523. Have alternatives been defined in the event that failure occurs?

524. Is there a set of procedures to capture, analyze and act on quality metrics?

525. The metrics–what is being considered?

526. Have risk areas been identified?

527. What does this tell us?

528. How effective are your security tests?

529. Were number of defects identified?

530. Does risk analysis documentation meet standards?

531. Are there any open risk issues?

532. Is a risk containment plan in place?

533. Are quality metrics defined?

534. How do you calculate corresponding metrics?

535. Is there alignment within your organization on definitions?

536. How can the effectiveness of each of the activities be measured?

537. What approved evidence based screening tools can be used?

538. Is quality culture a competitive advantage?

539. Were quality attributes reported?

2.26 Process Improvement Plan: CSSLP

540. What actions are needed to address the problems and achieve the goals?

541. Has the time line required to move measurement results from the points of collection to databases or users been established?

542. What makes people good SPI coaches?

543. If a process improvement framework is being used, which elements will help the problems and goals listed?

544. Who should prepare the process improvement action plan?

545. What personnel are the sponsors for that initiative?

546. What personnel are the change agents for your initiative?

547. Where are you now?

548. Why quality management?

549. Are you making progress on the improvement framework?

550. Are there forms and procedures to collect and

record the data?

551. Management commitment at all levels?

552. Everyone agrees on what process improvement is, right?

553. Have the frequency of collection and the points in the process where measurements will be made been determined?

554. The motive is determined by asking, Why do you want to achieve this goal?

555. Does your process ensure quality?

556. What is quality and how will you ensure it?

557. Are you meeting the quality standards?

558. What personnel are the coaches for your initiative?

559. How do you measure?

2.27 Responsibility Assignment Matrix: CSSLP

560. What happens when others get pulled for higher priority CSSLP projects?

561. Budgeted cost for work scheduled?

562. Changes in the nature of the overhead requirements?

563. Is work properly classified as measured effort, LOE, or apportioned effort and appropriately separated?

564. Are all elements of indirect expense identified to overhead cost budgets of CSSLP projections?

565. Is accountability placed at the lowest-possible level within the CSSLP project so that decisions can be made at that level?

566. Budgets assigned to major functional organizations?

567. Can the contractor substantiate work package and planning package budgets?

568. What expertise is available in your department?

569. Changes in the overhead pool and/or organization structures?

570. Does each activity-deliverable have exactly one Accountable responsibility, so that accountability is clear and decisions can be made quickly?

571. Changes in the current direct and CSSLP projected base?

572. Too many rs: with too many people labeled as doing the work, are there too many hands involved?

573. Is the entire contract planned in time-phased control accounts to the extent practicable?

574. Are the actual costs used for variance analysis reconcilable with data from the accounting system?

575. Major functional areas of contract effort?

576. Undistributed budgets, if any?

577. What do you do when people do not respond?

2.28 Roles and Responsibilities: CSSLP

578. Who is responsible for each task?

579. What specific behaviors did you observe?

580. What is working well?

581. Have you ever been a part of this team?

582. What areas of supervision are challenging for you?

583. Is there a training program in place for stakeholders covering expectations, roles and responsibilities and any addition knowledge others need to be good stakeholders?

584. What should you do now to prepare yourself for a promotion, increased responsibilities or a different job?

585. Do you take the time to clearly define roles and responsibilities on CSSLP project tasks?

586. Do the values and practices inherent in the culture of your organization foster or hinder the process?

587. What areas would you highlight for changes or improvements?

588. What are your major roles and responsibilities in the area of performance measurement and

assessment?

589. Are CSSLP project team roles and responsibilities identified and documented?

590. Who is involved?

591. What expectations were NOT met?

592. Are your policies supportive of a culture of quality data?

593. Concern: where are you limited or have no authority, where you can not influence?

594. Is the data complete?

595. Was the expectation clearly communicated?

596. Who is responsible for implementation activities and where will the functions, roles and responsibilities be defined?

597. Once the responsibilities are defined for the CSSLP project, have the deliverables, roles and responsibilities been clearly communicated to every participant?

2.29 Human Resource Management Plan: CSSLP

598. Have all documents been archived in a CSSLP project repository for each release?

599. Are updated CSSLP project time & resource estimates reasonable based on the current CSSLP project stage?

600. Is the current culture aligned with the vision, mission, and values of the department?

601. Were CSSLP project team members involved in the development of activity & task decomposition?

602. Have the key elements of a coherent CSSLP project management strategy been established?

603. Are all payments made according to the contract(s)?

604. Are procurement deliverables arriving on time and to specification?

605. How does the proposed individual meet each requirement?

606. Have stakeholder accountabilities & responsibilities been clearly defined?

607. What commitments have been made?

608. Are the people assigned to the CSSLP project sufficiently qualified?

609. Is the steering committee active in CSSLP project oversight?

610. Are risk triggers captured?

611. Are meeting objectives identified for each meeting?

612. Where is your organization headed?

2.30 Communications Management Plan: CSSLP

613. Who needs to know and how much?

614. What approaches to you feel are the best ones to use?

615. Timing: when do the effects of the communication take place?

616. Who is the stakeholder?

617. Why do you manage communications?

618. What steps can you take for a positive relationship?

619. What is CSSLP project communications management?

620. What is the stakeholders level of authority?

621. Do you then often overlook a key stakeholder or stakeholder group?

622. In your work, how much time is spent on stakeholder identification?

623. What are the interrelationships?

624. Who have you worked with in past, similar initiatives?

625. Is there an important stakeholder who is actively opposed and will not receive messages?

626. Why manage stakeholders?

627. Are there common objectives between the team and the stakeholder?

628. Do you feel a register helps?

629. Do you ask; can you recommend others for you to talk with about this initiative?

630. Can you think of other people who might have concerns or interests?

631. What communications method?

2.31 Risk Management Plan: CSSLP

632. Who/what can assist?

633. Are the metrics meaningful and useful?

634. Is security a central objective?

635. How can the process be made more effective or less cumbersome (process improvements)?

636. Do benefits and chances of success outweigh potential damage if success is not attained?

637. How is risk response planning performed?

638. Are flexibility and reuse paramount?

639. What worked well?

640. Where do risks appear in the business phases?

641. Are the reports useful and easy to read?

642. How much risk protection can you afford?

643. Is there anything you would now do differently on your CSSLP project based on this experience?

644. Was an original risk assessment/risk management plan completed?

645. How would you suggest monitoring for risk transition indicators?

646. Are staff committed for the duration of the product?

647. What risks are tracked?

648. Does the customer understand the software process?

649. My CSSLP project leader has suddenly left your organization, what do you do?

650. What can go wrong?

2.32 Risk Register: CSSLP

651. Recovery actions - planned actions taken once a risk has occurred to allow you to move on. What should you do after?

652. Market risk -will the new service or product be useful to your organization or marketable to others?

653. What are the major risks facing the CSSLP project?

654. Who is going to do it?

655. What is a Community Risk Register?

656. When would you develop a risk register?

657. What evidence do you have to justify the likelihood score of the risk (audit, incident report, claim, complaints, inspection, internal review)?

658. What could prevent you delivering on the strategic program objectives and what is being done to mitigate corresponding issues?

659. How is a Community Risk Register created?

660. How could corresponding Risk affect the CSSLP project in terms of cost and schedule?

661. What are the main aims, objectives of the policy, strategy, or service and the intended outcomes?

662. What action, if any, has been taken to respond to the risk?

663. What would the impact to the CSSLP project objectives be should the risk arise?

664. Have other controls and solutions been implemented in other services which could be applied as an alternative to additional funding?

665. Cost/benefit – how much will the proposed mitigations cost and how does this cost compare with the potential cost of the risk event/situation should it occur?

666. What are the assumptions and current status that support the assessment of the risk?

667. Risk documentation: what reporting formats and processes will be used for risk management activities?

668. Are there other alternative controls that could be implemented?

669. Severity Prediction?

670. What may happen or not go according to plan?

2.33 Probability and Impact Assessment: CSSLP

671. Is it necessary to deeply assess all CSSLP project risks?

672. What will be the environmental impact of the CSSLP project?

673. Are formal technical reviews part of this process?

674. What are the current requirements of the customer?

675. What is the level of experience available with your organization?

676. Will new information become available during the CSSLP project?

677. Are the facilities, expertise, resources, and management know-how available to handle the situation?

678. What are the industrial relations prevailing in your organization?

679. How is risk handled within this CSSLP project organization?

680. Do the people have the right combinations of skills?

681. Do you train all developers in the process?

682. What should be the external organizations responsibility vis-à-vis total stake in the CSSLP project?

683. Supply/demand CSSLP projections and trends; what are the levels of accuracy?

684. Are the software tools integrated with each other?

685. What things might go wrong?

686. What things are likely to change?

687. Assumptions analysis -what assumptions have you made or been given about your CSSLP project?

688. What is the probability of the risk occurring?

689. What are the current or emerging trends of culture?

2.34 Probability and Impact Matrix: CSSLP

690. Is the technology to be built new to your organization?

691. Are compilers and code generators available and suitable for the product to be built?

692. Do the requirements require the creation of new algorithms?

693. What is the likelihood of a breakthrough?

694. Are some people working on multiple CSSLP projects?

695. What action do you usually take against risks?

696. How well is the risk understood?

697. What risks are necessary to achieve success?

698. How carefully have the potential competitors been identified?

699. Can it be enlarged by drawing people from other areas of your organization?

700. What action would you take to the identified risks in the CSSLP project?

701. My CSSLP project leader has suddenly left your

organization, what do you do?

702. What will the damage be?

703. The customer requests a change to the CSSLP project that would increase the CSSLP project risk. Which should you do before ass the others?

704. How will economic events and trends likely affect the CSSLP project?

705. Can it be changed quickly?

706. Do you manage the process through use of metrics?

707. What is the risk appetite?

708. Degree of confidence in estimated size estimate?

2.35 Risk Data Sheet: CSSLP

709. What are you trying to achieve (Objectives)?

710. What can you do?

711. What is the environment within which you operate (social trends, economic, community values, broad based participation, national directions etc.)?

712. Has a sensitivity analysis been carried out?

713. How can it happen?

714. Type of risk identified?

715. Do effective diagnostic tests exist?

716. What actions can be taken to eliminate or remove risk?

717. What are you weak at and therefore need to do better?

718. Has the most cost-effective solution been chosen?

719. What were the Causes that contributed?

720. Is the data sufficiently specified in terms of the type of failure being analyzed, and its frequency or probability?

721. What is the likelihood of it happening?

722. What is the duration of infection (the length of time the host is infected with the organizm) in a normal healthy human host?

723. If it happens, what are the consequences?

724. What is the chance that it will happen?

725. Are new hazards created?

726. What can happen?

727. What if client refuses?

728. How do you handle product safely?

2.36 Procurement Management Plan: CSSLP

729. Is the steering committee active in CSSLP project oversight?

730. Are issues raised, assessed, actioned, and resolved in a timely and efficient manner?

731. Are staff skills known and available for each task?

732. Are change requests logged and managed?

733. Are CSSLP project team roles and responsibilities identified and documented?

734. Was the CSSLP project schedule reviewed by all stakeholders and formally accepted?

735. Are the payment terms being followed?

736. Are the CSSLP project team members located locally to the users/stakeholders?

737. Is there a formal process for updating the CSSLP project baseline?

738. Is stakeholder involvement adequate?

739. Are changes in deliverable commitments agreed to by all affected groups & individuals?

740. Are action items captured and managed?

741. Have all unresolved risks been documented?

742. Does the resource management plan include a personnel development plan?

2.37 Source Selection Criteria: CSSLP

743. Who is entitled to a debriefing?

744. What documentation is necessary regarding electronic communications?

745. What are the limitations on pre-competitive range communications?

746. What should be considered when developing evaluation standards?

747. Can you make a cost/technical tradeoff?

748. Can you reasonably estimate total organization requirements for the coming year?

749. If the costs are normalized, please account for how the normalization is conducted. Is a cost realism analysis used?

750. How is past performance evaluated?

751. Are responses to considerations adequate?

752. How important is cost in the source selection decision relative to past performance and technical considerations?

753. How long will it take for the purchase cost to be the same as the lease cost?

754. With the rapid changes in information

technology, will media be readable in five or ten years?

755. Is experience evaluated?

756. How can business terms and conditions be improved to yield more effective price competition?

757. Do you have a plan to document consensus results including disposition of any disagreement by individual evaluators?

758. What should clarifications include?

759. What are the requirements for publicizing a RFP?

760. What are the guidelines regarding award without considerations?

761. When is it appropriate to conduct a preproposal conference?

762. When and what information can be considered with offerors regarding past performance?

2.38 Stakeholder Management Plan: CSSLP

763. What are the criteria for selecting suppliers of off the shelf products?

764. Is the performance of the supplier to be rated and documented?

765. Have all involved stakeholders and work groups committed to the CSSLP project?

766. Have process improvement efforts been completed before requirements efforts begin?

767. Are non-critical path items updated and agreed upon with the teams?

768. What process was used to identify risks to the CSSLP projects success?

769. Are the CSSLP project team members located locally to the users/stakeholders?

770. What is the process for purchases that arent acceptable (eg damaged goods)?

771. How are the overall CSSLP project development processes to be undertaken to produce the CSSLP project outputs?

772. Has a provision been made to reassess CSSLP project risks at various CSSLP project stages?

773. Is there any form of automated support for Issues Management?

774. Are communication systems currently in place appropriate?

775. Is the CSSLP project sponsor clearly communicating the business case or rationale for why this CSSLP project is needed?

776. In your opinion, do certain CSSLP project resources hold a higher importance than other resources?

777. Are the quality tools and methods identified in the Quality Plan appropriate to the CSSLP project?

778. What guidelines or procedures currently exist that must be adhered to (eg departmental accounting procedures)?

779. Will all outputs delivered by the CSSLP project follow the same process?

780. How many CSSLP project staff does this specific process affect?

781. Are corrective actions and variances reported?

2.39 Change Management Plan: CSSLP

782. What is the reason for the communication?

783. Is there an adequate supply of people for the new roles?

784. How can you best frame the message so that it addresses the audiences interests?

785. What time commitment will this involve?

786. How do you know the requirements you documented are the right ones?

787. What prerequisite knowledge do corresponding groups need?

788. Who is the audience for change management activities?

789. How many people are required in each of the roles?

790. Has this been negotiated with the customer and sponsor?

791. What is the negative impact of communicating too soon or too late?

792. What do you expect the target audience to do, say, think or feel as a result of this communication?

793. What new competencies will be required for the roles?

794. Is there a need for new relationships to be built?

795. How badly can information be misinterpreted?

796. What is going to be done differently?

797. What can you do to minimise misinterpretation and negative perceptions?

798. Are there resource implications for your communications strategy?

799. Identify the risk and assess the significance and likelihood of it occurring and plan the contingency What risks may occur upfront?

800. How much CSSLP project management is needed?

3.0 Executing Process Group: CSSLP

801. Do the partners have sufficient financial capacity to keep up the benefits produced by the programme?

802. Will additional funds be needed for hardware or software?

803. How could you control progress of your CSSLP project?

804. Do the products created live up to the necessary quality?

805. How will professionals learn what is expected from them what the deliverables are?

806. What were things that you did very well and want to do the same again on the next CSSLP project?

807. What is the critical path for this CSSLP project and how long is it?

808. Will outside resources be needed to help?

809. Are the necessary foundations in place to ensure the sustainability of the results of the programme?

810. It under budget or over budget?

811. Is the schedule for the set products being met?

812. What areas does the group agree are the biggest success on the CSSLP project?

813. When will the CSSLP project be done?

814. How well did the chosen processes fit the needs of the CSSLP project?

815. What communication items need improvement?

816. What will you do to minimize the impact should a risk event occur?

817. Is the CSSLP project performing better or worse than planned?

818. Do schedule issues conflicts?

819. What is in place for ensuring adequate change control on CSSLP projects that involve outside contracts?

3.1 Team Member Status Report: CSSLP

820. Why is it to be done?

821. Is there evidence that staff is taking a more professional approach toward management of your organizations CSSLP projects?

822. How will resource planning be done?

823. How does this product, good, or service meet the needs of the CSSLP project and your organization as a whole?

824. How it is to be done?

825. Does the product, good, or service already exist within your organization?

826. Does your organization have the means (staff, money, contract, etc.) to produce or to acquire the product, good, or service?

827. Will the staff do training or is that done by a third party?

828. Do you have an Enterprise CSSLP project Management Office (EPMO)?

829. What is to be done?

830. The problem with Reward & Recognition

Programs is that the truly deserving people all too often get left out. How can you make it practical?

831. Are the products of your organizations CSSLP projects meeting customers objectives?

832. When a teams productivity and success depend on collaboration and the efficient flow of information, what generally fails them?

833. How can you make it practical?

834. Does every department have to have a CSSLP project Manager on staff?

835. Are your organizations CSSLP projects more successful over time?

836. How much risk is involved?

837. Are the attitudes of staff regarding CSSLP project work improving?

838. What specific interest groups do you have in place?

3.2 Change Request: CSSLP

839. Who is responsible for the implementation and monitoring of all measures?

840. Has your address changed?

841. What mechanism is used to appraise others of changes that are made?

842. Describe how modifications, enhancements, defects and/or deficiencies shall be notified (e.g. Problem Reports, Change Requests etc) and managed. Detail warranty and/or maintenance periods?

843. How are the measures for carrying out the change established?

844. What is the purpose of change control?

845. Will all change requests and current status be logged?

846. Who is communicating the change?

847. What are the requirements for urgent changes?

848. Who is responsible to authorize changes?

849. What should be regulated in a change control operating instruction?

850. Should a more thorough impact analysis be

conducted?

851. Will all change requests be unconditionally tracked through this process?

852. When do you create a change request?

853. What must be taken into consideration when introducing change control programs?

854. Who needs to approve change requests?

855. How fast will change requests be approved?

856. Who can suggest changes?

857. When to submit a change request?

858. How can changes be graded?

3.3 Change Log: CSSLP

859. Who initiated the change request?

860. Is the submitted change a new change or a modification of a previously approved change?

861. Is the change request open, closed or pending?

862. How does this change affect the timeline of the schedule?

863. Where do changes come from?

864. When was the request submitted?

865. Is the change request within CSSLP project scope?

866. Is the requested change request a result of changes in other CSSLP project(s)?

867. Is the change backward compatible without limitations?

868. How does this change affect scope?

869. Is this a mandatory replacement?

870. Will the CSSLP project fail if the change request is not executed?

871. Do the described changes impact on the integrity or security of the system?

872. When was the request approved?

873. How does this relate to the standards developed for specific business processes?

3.4 Decision Log: CSSLP

874. With whom was the decision shared or considered?

875. Which variables make a critical difference?

876. Who is the decisionmaker?

877. Do strategies and tactics aimed at less than full control reduce the costs of management or simply shift the cost burden?

878. How does the use a Decision Support System influence the strategies/tactics or costs?

879. How does provision of information, both in terms of content and presentation, influence acceptance of alternative strategies?

880. What is the average size of your matters in an applicable measurement?

881. What makes you different or better than others companies selling the same thing?

882. How does an increasing emphasis on cost containment influence the strategies and tactics used?

883. What is the line where eDiscovery ends and document review begins?

884. What was the rationale for the decision?

885. What alternatives/risks were considered?

886. What eDiscovery problem or issue did your organization set out to fix or make better?

887. How consolidated and comprehensive a story can you tell by capturing currently available incident data in a central location and through a log of key decisions during an incident?

888. Linked to original objective?

889. Decision-making process; how will the team make decisions?

890. At what point in time does loss become unacceptable?

891. Adversarial environment. is your opponent open to a non-traditional workflow, or will it likely challenge anything you do?

892. Meeting purpose; why does this team meet?

893. How effective is maintaining the log at facilitating organizational learning?

3.5 Quality Audit: CSSLP

894. Is your organizational structure established and each positions responsibility defined?

895. How does your organization know that the research supervision provided to its staff is appropriately effective and constructive?

896. How does your organization know whether they are adhering to mission and achieving objectives?

897. How does your organization know that its system for inducting new staff to maximize workplace contributions are appropriately effective and constructive?

898. How does your organization know that the system for managing its facilities is appropriately effective and constructive?

899. Does everyone know what they are supposed to be doing, how and why?

900. How does the organization know that its system for maintaining and advancing the capabilities of its staff, particularly in relation to the Mission of the organization, is appropriately effective and constructive?

901. What does the organizarion look for in a Quality audit?

902. How does your organization know that its

advisory services are appropriately effective and constructive?

903. How does your organization know that its relationships with industry and employers are appropriately effective and constructive?

904. What has changed/improved as a result of the review processes?

905. How does your organization know that its support services planning and management systems are appropriately effective and constructive?

906. What review processes are in place for your organizations major activities?

907. How does your organization know that its staff have appropriate access to a fair and effective grievance process?

908. How do you indicate the extent to which your personnel would be expected to contribute to the work effort?

909. Are complaint files maintained?

910. Are the intentions consistent with external obligations (such as applicable laws)?

911. How does the organization know that its industry and community engagement planning and management systems are appropriately effective and constructive in enabling relationships with key stakeholder groups?

912. How do you know what, specifically, is required of you in your work?

913. Are training programs documented?

3.6 Team Directory: CSSLP

914. Process decisions: do job conditions warrant additional actions to collect job information and document on-site activity?

915. Decisions: what could be done better to improve the quality of the constructed product?

916. How do unidentified risks impact the outcome of the CSSLP project?

917. How and in what format should information be presented?

918. Contract requirements complied with?

919. Where should the information be distributed?

920. Days from the time the issue is identified?

921. Do purchase specifications and configurations match requirements?

922. Who will report CSSLP project status to all stakeholders?

923. Where will the product be used and/or delivered or built when appropriate?

924. Does a CSSLP project team directory list all resources assigned to the CSSLP project?

925. Who are the Team Members?

926. When will you produce deliverables?

927. Why is the work necessary?

928. Process decisions: are contractors adequately prosecuting the work?

929. How will you accomplish and manage the objectives?

930. Decisions: is the most suitable form of contract being used?

931. Timing: when do the effects of communication take place?

932. Who should receive information (all stakeholders)?

3.7 Team Operating Agreement: CSSLP

933. What individual strengths does each team member bring to the group?

934. Have you established procedures that team members can follow to work effectively together, such as a team operating agreement?

935. Did you recap the meeting purpose, time, and expectations?

936. Communication protocols: how will the team communicate?

937. Resource allocation: how will individual team members account for time and expenses, and how will this be allocated in the team budget?

938. Do you ensure that all participants know how to use the required technology?

939. Are there more than two native languages represented by your team?

940. Do you use a parking lot for any items that are important and outside of the agenda?

941. What is your unique contribution to your organization?

942. Seconds for members to respond?

943. Do you call or email participants to ensure understanding, follow-through and commitment to the meeting outcomes?

944. What administrative supports will be put in place to support the team and the teams supervisor?

945. Are team roles clearly defined and accepted?

946. Must your team members rely on the expertise of other members to complete tasks?

947. Are there influences outside the team that may affect performance, and if so, have you identified and addressed them?

948. Do you listen for voice tone and word choice to understand the meaning behind words?

949. Did you delegate tasks such as taking meeting minutes, presenting a topic and soliciting input?

950. How will you resolve conflict efficiently and respectfully?

3.8 Team Performance Assessment: CSSLP

951. How do you encourage members to learn from each other?

952. How hard do you try to make a good selection?

953. What structural changes have you made or are you preparing to make?

954. To what degree do members understand and articulate the same purpose without relying on ambiguous abstractions?

955. Delaying market entry: how long is too long?

956. Do you give group members authority to make at least some important decisions?

957. Does more radicalness mean more perceived benefits?

958. Is there a particular method of data analysis that you would recommend as a means of demonstrating that method variance is not of great concern for a given dataset?

959. To what degree are the goals realistic?

960. When does the medium matter?

961. How much interpersonal friction is there in your

team?

962. To what degree are sub-teams possible or necessary?

963. To what degree does the teams purpose contain themes that are particularly meaningful and memorable?

964. To what degree does the team possess adequate membership to achieve its ends?

965. To what degree are the relative importance and priority of the goals clear to all team members?

966. How do you keep key people outside the group informed about its accomplishments?

967. Effects of crew composition on crew performance: Does the whole equal the sum of its parts?

968. To what degree does the teams purpose constitute a broader, deeper aspiration than just accomplishing short-term goals?

969. To what degree are the members clear on what they are individually responsible for and what they are jointly responsible for?

970. How do you recognize and praise members for contributions?

3.9 Team Member Performance Assessment: CSSLP

971. What is the large, desired outcome?

972. What changes do you need to make to align practices with beliefs?

973. What is collaboration?

974. What are the basic principles and objectives of performance measurement and assessment?

975. How will they be formed?

976. How is assessment information achieved, stored?

977. Why do performance reviews?

978. Verify business objectives. Are they appropriate, and well-articulated?

979. To what degree are the skill areas critical to team performance present?

980. What tools are available to determine whether all contract functional and compliance areas of performance objectives, measures, and incentives have been met?

981. Does the rater (supervisor) have the authority or responsibility to tell an employee that the employees performance is unsatisfactory?

982. What are the standards or expectations for success?

983. Did training work?

984. How do you know that all team members are learning?

985. How will you identify your Team Leaders?

986. What are acceptable governance changes?

987. To what degree are the teams goals and objectives clear, simple, and measurable?

988. Goals met?

989. To what degree do all members feel responsible for all agreed-upon measures?

990. What are they responsible for?

3.10 Issue Log: CSSLP

991. How much time does it take to do it?

992. What is a Stakeholder?

993. What does the stakeholder need from the team?

994. Are you constantly rushing from meeting to meeting?

995. What steps can you take for positive relationships?

996. What are the stakeholders interrelationships?

997. How do you manage communications?

998. Do you prepare stakeholder engagement plans?

999. What is the stakeholders political influence?

1000. Is access to the Issue Log controlled?

1001. How do you manage human resources?

1002. Who reported the issue?

1003. Who is involved as you identify stakeholders?

1004. Which stakeholders can influence others?

1005. What is the impact on the risks?

1006. Do you have members of your team responsible for certain stakeholders?

1007. Why do you manage human resources?

4.0 Monitoring and Controlling Process Group: CSSLP

1008. Are the services being delivered?

1009. Is there undesirable impact on staff or resources?

1010. What factors are contributing to progress or delay in the achievement of products and results?

1011. How well did the chosen processes produce the expected results?

1012. Did you implement the program as designed?

1013. Based on your CSSLP project communication management plan, what worked well?

1014. Contingency planning. if a risk event occurs, what will you do?

1015. Is the verbiage used appropriate and understandable?

1016. What good practices or successful experiences or transferable examples have been identified?

1017. Is the program making progress in helping to achieve the set results?

1018. What is the expected monetary value of the CSSLP project?

1019. What areas does the group agree are the biggest success on the CSSLP project?

1020. Feasibility: how much money, time, and effort can you put into this?

1021. Did the CSSLP project team have the right skills?

1022. How were collaborations developed, and how are they sustained?

1023. Who are the CSSLP project stakeholders?

1024. Is there sufficient time allotted between the general system design and the detailed system design phases?

1025. How is agile portfolio management done?

1026. Were decisions made in a timely manner?

4.1 Project Performance Report: CSSLP

1027. To what degree does the formal organization make use of individual resources and meet individual needs?

1028. To what degree do the structures of the formal organization motivate taskrelevant behavior and facilitate task completion?

1029. To what degree is there a sense that only the team can succeed?

1030. To what degree is the team cognizant of small wins to be celebrated along the way?

1031. To what degree will the team adopt a concrete, clearly understood, and agreed-upon approach that will result in achievement of the teams goals?

1032. How is the data used?

1033. To what degree will new and supplemental skills be introduced as the need is recognized?

1034. To what degree do team members understand one anothers roles and skills?

1035. To what degree can team members vigorously define the teams purpose in considerations with others who are not part of the functioning team?

1036. To what degree are fresh input and perspectives systematically caught and added (for example, through information and analysis, new members, and senior sponsors)?

1037. To what degree does the informal organization make use of individual resources and meet individual needs?

1038. To what degree do team members agree with the goals, relative importance, and the ways in which achievement will be measured?

1039. To what degree will the team ensure that all members equitably share the work essential to the success of the team?

1040. To what degree do individual skills and abilities match task demands?

1041. To what degree are the demands of the task compatible with and converge with the mission and functions of the formal organization?

4.2 Variance Analysis: CSSLP

1042. What should management do?

1043. Who are responsible for overhead performance control of related costs?

1044. Are all budgets assigned to control accounts?

1045. Are data elements reconcilable between internal summary reports and reports forwarded to the stakeholders?

1046. Did your organization lose existing customers and/or gain new customers?

1047. Budget versus actual. how does the monthly budget compare to actual experience?

1048. Does the contractors system provide unit or lot costs when applicable?

1049. Are records maintained to show how management reserves are used?

1050. Are there changes in the overhead pool and/or organization structures?

1051. Do you identify potential or actual budget-based and time-based schedule variances?

1052. Are indirect costs charged to the appropriate indirect pools and incurring organization?

1053. Historical experience?

1054. Are indirect costs accumulated for comparison with the corresponding budgets?

1055. How do you identify and isolate causes of favorable and unfavorable cost and schedule variances?

1056. Are procedures for variance analysis documented and consistently applied at the control account level and selected WBS and organizational levels at least monthly as a routine task?

1057. Wbs elements contractually specified for reporting of status to your organization (lowest level only)?

1058. Who are responsible for the establishment of budgets and assignment of resources for overhead performance?

1059. The anticipated business volume?

1060. Are the bases and rates for allocating costs from each indirect pool consistently applied?

4.3 Earned Value Status: CSSLP

1061. Verification is a process of ensuring that the developed system satisfies the stakeholders agreements and specifications; Are you building the product right? What do you verify?

1062. What is the unit of forecast value?

1063. Are you hitting your CSSLP projects targets?

1064. Earned value can be used in almost any CSSLP project situation and in almost any CSSLP project environment. it may be used on large CSSLP projects, medium sized CSSLP projects, tiny CSSLP projects (in cut-down form), complex and simple CSSLP projects and in any market sector. some people, of course, know all about earned value, they have used it for years - but perhaps not as effectively as they could have?

1065. How much is it going to cost by the finish?

1066. How does this compare with other CSSLP projects?

1067. If earned value management (EVM) is so good in determining the true status of a CSSLP project and CSSLP project its completion, why is it that hardly any one uses it in information systems related CSSLP projects?

1068. When is it going to finish?

1069. Validation is a process of ensuring that the developed system will actually achieve the stakeholders desired outcomes; Are you building the right product? What do you validate?

1070. Where are your problem areas?

1071. Where is evidence-based earned value in your organization reported?

4.4 Risk Audit: CSSLP

1072. Have you considered the health and safety of everyone in your organization and do you meet work health and safety regulations?

1073. Do all coaches/instructors/leaders have appropriate and current accreditation?

1074. How do you compare to other jurisdictions when managing the risk of ....?

1075. Level of preparation and skill?

1076. Have you worked with the customer in the past?

1077. Are enough people available?

1078. Can assurance be expanded beyond the traditional audit without undermining independence?

1079. How do you prioritize risks?

1080. Strategic business risk audit methodologies; are corresponding an attempt to sell other services, and is management becoming the client of the audit rather than the shareholder?

1081. Are your rules, by-laws and practices non-discriminatory?

1082. For this risk .. what do you need to stop doing, start doing and keep doing?

1083. What does monitoring consist of?

1084. How are risk appetites expressed?

1085. Auditor independence: a burdensome constraint or a core value?

1086. Does willful intent modify risk-based auditing?

1087. What are the boundaries of the auditors responsibility for policing management fidelity?

1088. Who is responsible for what?

1089. Is the process supported by tools?

1090. Are you aware of the industry standards that apply to your operations?

4.5 Contractor Status Report: CSSLP

1091. Who can list a CSSLP project as organization experience, your organization or a previous employee of your organization?

1092. What is the average response time for answering a support call?

1093. How is risk transferred?

1094. What are the minimum and optimal bandwidth requirements for the proposed soluiton?

1095. If applicable; describe your standard schedule for new software version releases. Are new software version releases included in the standard maintenance plan?

1096. What was the overall budget or estimated cost?

1097. Are there contractual transfer concerns?

1098. What was the final actual cost?

1099. What was the actual budget or estimated cost for your organizations services?

1100. Describe how often regular updates are made to the proposed solution. Are corresponding regular updates included in the standard maintenance plan?

1101. What process manages the contracts?

1102. What was the budget or estimated cost for your organizations services?

1103. How long have you been using the services?

4.6 Formal Acceptance: CSSLP

1104. Do you buy-in installation services?

1105. What can you do better next time?

1106. Was the client satisfied with the CSSLP project results?

1107. Does it do what CSSLP project team said it would?

1108. What function(s) does it fill or meet?

1109. Does it do what client said it would?

1110. What lessons were learned about your CSSLP project management methodology?

1111. Have all comments been addressed?

1112. Was the CSSLP project work done on time, within budget, and according to specification?

1113. Do you perform formal acceptance or burn-in tests?

1114. Who supplies data?

1115. Do you buy pre-configured systems or build your own configuration?

1116. How does your team plan to obtain formal acceptance on your CSSLP project?

1117. Did the CSSLP project manager and team act in a professional and ethical manner?

1118. General estimate of the costs and times to complete the CSSLP project?

1119. Did the CSSLP project achieve its MOV?

1120. What is the Acceptance Management Process?

1121. Was the CSSLP project managed well?

1122. Was business value realized?

1123. What are the requirements against which to test, Who will execute?

5.0 Closing Process Group: CSSLP

1124. Based on your CSSLP project communication management plan, what worked well?

1125. What level of risk does the proposed budget represent to the CSSLP project?

1126. How well did you do?

1127. What could have been improved?

1128. Is there a clear cause and effect between the activity and the lesson learned?

1129. If a risk event occurs, what will you do?

1130. What is the CSSLP project name and date of completion?

1131. Were sponsors and decision makers available when needed outside regularly scheduled meetings?

1132. What was learned?

1133. Is the CSSLP project funded?

1134. Were cost budgets met?

1135. What business situation is being addressed?

1136. What is the amount of funding and what CSSLP project phases are funded?

1137. Are there funding or time constraints?

1138. Did you do things well?

1139. How will you know you did it?

5.1 Procurement Audit: CSSLP

1140. Were additional works strictly necessary for the completion of performance under the contract?

1141. Are employees with cash disbursement responsibilities required to take scheduled vacations?

1142. Is there a practice that prohibits signing blank purchase orders?

1143. Is free and fair (international) competition promoted by organizational policies and legislation, in line with legal, trade organizations and other policies?

1144. Are there systems for recording and managing stocks (where part of contract)?

1145. Were additional works brought about by a cause which had not previously existed?

1146. When tenders were actually rejected because they were abnormally low, were reasons for this decision given and were they sufficiently grounded?

1147. Is a risk evaluation performed?

1148. Are fixed asset accounts posted currently?

1149. Has your organization taken a well-grounded decision about the procurement procedure chosen and has it documented the process?

1150. Does procurement staff have recognized professional procurement qualifications or sufficient training?

1151. Were the documents received scrutinised for completion and adherence to stated conditions before the tenders were evaluated?

1152. Is it on a regular basis examined whether it is possible to enter into public private partnerships with private suppliers?

1153. Has the department identified and described the different elements in the procurement process?

1154. Can small orders such as magazine subscriptions and non-product items such as membership in organizations be processed by the ordering department?

1155. Are there procedures for trade-in arrangements?

1156. Does the strategy ensure that appropriate controls are in place to ensure propriety and regularity in delivery?

1157. Are the supporting documents for payments voided or cancelled following payment?

1158. Is your organization transparent about winning bids and prices?

1159. Was there a sound basis for the scorings applied to the criteria and was the scoring well balanced?

5.2 Contract Close-Out: CSSLP

1160. How is the contracting office notified of the automatic contract close-out?

1161. Parties: who is involved?

1162. What happens to the recipient of services?

1163. How/when used ?

1164. Have all contracts been closed?

1165. Have all acceptance criteria been met prior to final payment to contractors?

1166. Was the contract type appropriate?

1167. Was the contract sufficiently clear so as not to result in numerous disputes and misunderstandings?

1168. Are the signers the authorized officials?

1169. Change in attitude or behavior?

1170. Change in circumstances?

1171. Change in knowledge?

1172. Have all contract records been included in the CSSLP project archives?

1173. How does it work?

1174. What is capture management?

1175. Has each contract been audited to verify acceptance and delivery?

1176. Have all contracts been completed?

1177. Parties: Authorized?

1178. Was the contract complete without requiring numerous changes and revisions?

5.3 Project or Phase Close-Out: CSSLP

1179. What are the mandatory communication needs for each stakeholder?

1180. Planned completion date?

1181. What was the preferred delivery mechanism?

1182. In preparing the Lessons Learned report, should it reflect a consensus viewpoint, or should the report reflect the different individual viewpoints?

1183. What are the marketing communication needs for each stakeholder?

1184. What were the desired outcomes?

1185. Who are the CSSLP project stakeholders and what are roles and involvement?

1186. Were messages directly related to the release strategy or phases of the CSSLP project?

1187. What are the informational communication needs for each stakeholder?

1188. What is a Risk Management Process?

1189. Were risks identified and mitigated?

1190. Who controlled key decisions that were made?

1191. What security considerations needed to be

addressed during the procurement life cycle?

1192. Can the lesson learned be replicated?

1193. What advantages do the an individual interview have over a group meeting, and vice-versa?

1194. What can you do better next time, and what specific actions can you take to improve?

1195. Does the lesson describe a function that would be done differently the next time?

1196. What hierarchical authority does the stakeholder have in your organization?

1197. Was the user/client satisfied with the end product?

5.4 Lessons Learned: CSSLP

1198. Is the lesson significant, valid, and applicable?

1199. Overall, how effective was the performance of the CSSLP project Manager?

1200. How well were CSSLP project issues communicated throughout your involvement in the CSSLP project?

1201. Was any formal risk assessment carried out at the start of the CSSLP project, and was this followed up during the CSSLP project?

1202. Is the lesson based on actual CSSLP project experience rather than on independent research?

1203. Was there a CSSLP project Definition document. Was there a CSSLP project Plan. Were they used during the CSSLP project?

1204. How useful was your testing?

1205. What was the single greatest success and the single greatest shortcoming or challenge from the CSSLP projects perspective?

1206. What was the geopolitical history during the origin of your organization and at the time of task input?

1207. What would you like to see better documented about how to use existing processes on this type of

CSSLP project?

1208. Was sufficient time allocated to review CSSLP project deliverables?

1209. What should have been accomplished during predeployment that was not accomplished?

1210. How well prepared were you to receive CSSLP project deliverables?

1211. How to write up the lesson identified – how will you document the results of your analysis corresponding that you have an li ready to take the next step in the ll process?

1212. Did the CSSLP project management methodology work?

1213. How clearly defined were the objectives for this CSSLP project?

1214. Was the control overhead justified?

1215. How was the CSSLP project controlled?

1216. How well was CSSLP project status communicated throughout your involvement in the CSSLP project?

Index

called 40, 137
cancelled   256
cannot123, 156, 166, 176
capability   20, 28, 40, 88, 116, 132, 151, 182
capable   7, 33
capacities   137
capacity   20, 132, 216
capital85, 91
capture   95, 152, 186, 258
captured   40, 141, 157, 195, 208
capturing   225
career 147
carefully   204
carried111, 206, 261
carrying   220
cash-drain   135
Cashflow   135
catalog   123
categories   40, 112
caught242
caused   1, 49
causes 42, 46, 50-51, 55, 60, 88, 206, 244
causing   18, 152
celebrated   241
center 52
central198, 225
certain 78, 130, 213, 238
certified   158
certifying   45
chaired   8
challenge   7, 112, 225, 261
challenges   72, 105, 125, 163
champion   27
chance   207
chances   198
change   5, 17, 35, 53-54, 60, 70, 75-76, 100, 110, 133-134, 142, 150, 153, 161, 166, 171, 176, 182-183, 188, 203, 205, 208, 214, 217, 220-222, 257
changed   21, 35, 86, 130, 176, 180, 182-183, 205, 220, 227
changes   63, 75, 77, 79, 82, 89, 92, 112-113, 120, 131, 141-142, 144, 149, 156, 169, 183, 190-192, 208, 210, 220-222, 233, 235-236, 243, 258
charged   243

management 1, 3-5, 9, 11-12, 21, 28, 34-36, 51, 53, 59, 61, 68, 72-74, 76, 90, 95, 104-105, 109, 113, 115-116, 120-121, 123, 130, 135, 138-139, 141-143, 149-151, 156-157, 173, 175, 177, 182, 184-185, 188-189, 194, 196, 198, 201-202, 208-209, 212-215, 218, 224, 227, 239-240, 243, 245, 247-248, 251-253, 258-259, 262

manager 7, 11, 18, 30, 34, 108, 219, 252, 261
managers 2, 129, 171-172
manages 249
managing 2, 129, 134, 144, 226, 247, 255
mandate 135
mandatory 222, 259
manner 155, 208, 240, 252
manual 21, 51, 71, 109
mapped 28
margin 157
marked 149
market 21, 118, 132, 135, 163, 200, 233, 245
marketable 200
marketer 7
marketing 43, 259
massively 53
material 80, 155-156
materials 1, 101
matrices 147
Matrix 3-4, 135, 147-148, 190, 204
matter 34, 233
matters 224
maturity 73
maximize 226
maximum 127
meaning 161, 232
meaningful 43, 198, 234
measurable 27, 35, 132, 178, 236
measure 2, 12, 18, 22, 32, 37-38, 40-48, 55-56, 59, 62, 67, 77, 81, 84-85, 93, 138, 150, 180, 184, 186, 189
measured 41, 43, 46, 86, 184-185, 187, 190, 242
measures 40, 45, 47-48, 51, 56, 60, 63, 68, 78, 86, 89, 220, 235-236
mechanical 1
mechanism 152, 220, 259
mechanisms 138
medium 233, 245
meeting 35, 89, 189, 195, 219, 225, 231-232, 237, 260

perform   27, 31, 33, 46, 51, 95, 104, 126, 139, 143, 159, 172, 251
performed   58, 68, 72, 75, 81, 103, 115, 147, 159, 177, 198, 255
performing   217
performs   34, 40
perhaps   102, 245
period 34, 79, 155
periodic   103, 177
periods 220
permission   1
permit 49
person 1, 17, 19
personally   147
personnel   21, 92, 100, 158, 166, 176, 188-189, 209, 227
pertinent   92
phases 44, 58, 68, 75, 82, 198, 240, 253, 259
physical   58
pieces 54
placed 190
planned   41, 43, 93, 95, 156, 161, 173, 177, 191, 200, 217, 259
planners   92
planning   3, 9, 86-87, 90, 92, 131, 137, 139, 149-150, 165, 167, 169, 171, 190, 198, 218, 227, 239
platform   70, 103
please 210
pocket 180
pockets   180
points 23, 37, 49, 65, 81, 83, 96, 128, 163, 188-189
poking 172
policies   53, 100, 108, 114, 122, 136, 193, 255
policing   248
policy 29, 92, 109, 136, 151, 167, 200
political   78, 237
poorly 31, 68, 77
portfolio   108, 240
portray 55
positioned   180-181
positions   226
positive   63, 196, 237
possess 69, 234
possible   42, 55, 60, 74, 84, 116, 141, 234, 256

problems   20, 42, 44-45, 49, 70, 77, 88, 149, 188
procedure   71, 255
procedures   11, 46, 53, 65, 89-90, 95, 99, 108, 142, 151, 167,
176, 178, 183-186, 188, 213, 231, 244, 256
proceed   93, 155
process   1-7, 11, 26-27, 29-30, 36-38, 40-44, 48, 50-65, 70,
79-80, 84-86, 88-90, 93-95, 130, 137-139, 141, 143, 147, 149-152,
157, 167, 171-172, 184, 188-189, 192, 198-199, 202-203, 205, 208,
212-213, 216, 221, 225, 227, 229-230, 239, 245-246, 248-249, 252-
253, 255-256, 259, 262
processed   56, 60, 256
processes   28, 40, 53, 56-57, 59, 61-65, 89, 130, 137, 142, 149,
201, 212, 217, 223, 227, 239, 261
processing   53, 58
processor   56
produce   137, 167, 212, 218, 230, 239
produced   216
produces   161
producing   147
product   1, 11, 19, 34, 40, 51, 57, 63, 72-74, 77, 81, 85-87,
89, 93, 100-102, 106, 111, 117, 123-124, 126, 132, 163, 175, 182,
199-200, 204, 207, 218, 229, 245-246, 260
production   41, 68, 72, 101, 116
productive   68
products   1, 18, 23, 36, 52, 55, 59, 132, 137-138, 147, 158,
178, 183, 212, 216, 219, 239
program   19, 47, 108, 110, 120, 124-125, 132, 137-138, 192,
200, 239
programme   216
programs   172, 219, 221, 228
progress   33, 85, 92, 131, 138, 150, 180, 188, 216, 239
prohibited   156
prohibits   255
project 2-7, 9, 18, 30, 59, 61-62, 64-65, 76, 85-86, 89-91, 93, 95,
99, 102, 104, 111-115, 119, 129-132, 134-144, 146-147, 149-151,
153-154, 157-161, 163-166, 169, 171-177, 179-183, 190, 192-196,
198-205, 208, 212-213, 215-219, 222, 229, 239-241, 245, 249, 251-
253, 257, 259, 261-262
projected   191
projects   2, 49, 71, 86, 105, 115-116, 126, 129, 147, 154,
171-172, 175, 177, 179, 183-184, 190, 204, 212, 217-219, 245, 261
promises   118
promoted   255

required   18, 29, 31-35, 44, 52, 61, 77, 86, 131, 145, 159,
161-162, 174, 178, 188, 214-215, 228, 231, 255
requires   86, 89
requiring   134, 258
research   21, 226, 261
resemble   171
reserved   1
reserves   177, 243
residual   79, 82, 156
resolution   63, 150
resolve 43, 232
resolved   178, 208
Resource   3-4, 161, 167, 169, 194, 209, 215, 218, 231
resources   2, 9, 20, 26, 31, 44, 74, 77, 86, 94, 132, 146, 157,
159, 161-162, 166, 174, 176, 179-180, 183, 202, 213, 216, 229, 237-
239, 241-242, 244
respect   1
respond   191, 201, 231
responded   13
response   19, 21, 62, 71, 74, 78, 86-89, 93, 172, 198, 249
responses   210
responsive   113, 173, 180
result   54, 181, 214, 222, 227, 241, 257
resulted   96
resulting   64
results 9, 28, 63, 67, 73, 78, 81-82, 93, 137-138, 158, 171, 175,
181, 188, 211, 216, 239, 251, 262
Retain 97
retained   117
retention   34
retentions   117
retirement   98, 117, 127
return   40, 166
reused 120
review 11, 17, 64, 79, 103, 111, 119, 122, 165, 182, 200, 224, 227,
262
reviewed   26, 98, 118, 208
reviews 11, 102, 111, 114, 150, 157-158, 177, 202, 235
revised 60, 96
revisions   258
reward 46, 63, 218
rewards   89
rights   1, 17, 103

statement   3, 12, 77, 149, 152, 179, 183
statements   13, 23, 28, 35, 37, 49, 56, 66, 83, 96, 128, 143
static   99, 107, 114
statistics   149
status   5-6, 131, 135, 144, 155, 158, 201, 218, 220, 229, 244-245,
249, 262
steering   151, 195, 208
stocks 255
storage   19, 53, 99
stored 33, 235
strategic   33, 92, 200, 247
strategies   152, 177, 224
strategy   20, 100, 116, 120, 135, 177, 194, 200, 215, 256,
259
strengths   152, 163, 231
stress   124
strictly 255
string   122
strive   171
striving 132
Strongly   12, 17, 25, 38, 50, 67, 84, 97
structural   233
structure   3, 74, 113, 116, 149, 153-154, 156, 169, 226
structured   88
structures   190, 241, 243
subdivided   156
subject9-10, 34, 81
Subjective   186
submit 11, 221
submitted   11, 222
subscribe   88
subscript   122
subset 18
subsystem   105
sub-teams   234
subtotals   178
succeed   163, 241
success   17, 22, 31-32, 42-43, 46, 112, 116, 119, 130, 136,
157, 166, 171, 198, 204, 212, 216, 219, 236, 240, 242, 261
successful   70, 82, 93, 112, 219, 239
suddenly   199, 204
sufficient   42, 80, 216, 240, 256, 262
suggest   198, 221